SMRTi

Nina Zivancevic

SPUYTEN DUYVIL
New York City

ISBN 978-1-959556-29-9
Cover photo: Nina Z. in Orvietto, Italia, by Gary Brackett

Library of Congress Control Number: 2023943584

This book is dedicated to the luminous shadows
of the best anthropologists I've known so far:
Marcel Mauss, Cornelius Castoriadis,
my father Vladimir Zivancevic
and
to the one resembling them at their best:
David Graeber

INDIA

SMRTi[1]

December 2014-January 2015
Paris-Riyadh—Cochin—Jeddah—Paris

Thoughts about the entity called "Barbarogenius" haunted the usual posse of avant-garde writers, authors such as Ljubomir Micić and Henri Michaux. At the very dawn of that distant 1931, Michaux decided to leave behind the mentality of the colonizer, he went to India where he started writing the text "Barbarian in Asia." He felt himself to be a barbarian under the wing of an ancient civilization, perhaps marked by the same feeling that Antonin Artaud acquired in the early 1900s after visiting the big Colonial Exhibition in Paris. The exhibition changed not only his life but also his understanding of life as such and the arts.

Michaux: "I noticed a man on the street. He grabbed me, and I was not able to see anyone else, only him. I got attached to him. I followed him everywhere, persuaded that he was the only one who existed in this world. More precisely it was him and the flute player, and a man involved in theater, and the acrobat on a rope gesturing loudly, so in a split second

---

1. Smṛti : remembrance, a vyabhicāri-bhāva; revealed scriptures supplementary to the śruti, or original Vedic scriptures, which are the Vedas and Upaniṣads; scriptures compiled by living entities under transcendental direction
2. What is remembered, the secondary Vedic literatures, which need not be passed down verbatim but may be reworded by the sages who transmit them in each age
3. Quick passing of the recollected memories before one dies

(Sanskrit-English dictionary)

I observed them all and I understood everything there was to be understood."

Michaux would say then that either India, its peoples or its society, should ever succumb to the influence of Westerners. This statement attests to the nobility of his character: he was a "Westerner" himself. Whereas someone like me, a writer coming from the Balkans, could never boast of such nobility. Besides I could never have that domineering way with people.

A "Barbarogenius," that is, a simple barbarian I am, in image and in person. Or, rather, I was Tito's imaginary cousin, related to that late Yugoslav president who, accompanied by Nehru and Nasser, sought to build 'the third world,' that is the non-aligned world.

And by the end of his journey Michaux said: "I was observing myself during my journey as if I would observe someone else who was observing the world with emotion, remembering an imaginary land which he does not inhabit. I was not there, I did not even visit it."

Unlike Michaux, I have always lived there, barbarian that I am, I am a part of it, I was there even when I did not live in it.

AIRPORT

That very morning, before I set out on that trip, I turned on my TV and what did I see? A belated report on the devastating consequences of a Tsunami on the beaches of the Indian state of Kerala. These images were there to remind me that I was heading into some special zone on Earth. These images were already encapsulated by Tarkovsky in one of his science-fiction films. Yes, it was his very own, very special, interplanetary world. I began to wonder, right there in front of my TV: how is it possible that life continues after the Tsunami, and why weren't they evacuated. How did it happen that the villagers could not avoid that natural disaster? Why did they give up on life? And those who stayed, how could they have continued living there? Why not choose some other part of the world, some other and better soil?

With their eyes, refracted mirrors, their gaze fixed, falling down neither too low upon their soil nor straying too high up into the heavens, the Hindus meditate with their legs crossed, their bodies divided into seven chakras, in the lotus position. In their musings they get right next to the sky. They devote their early morning prayers as well as their late evening prayers to the goddess Kali, with persistence and certain pleasure which in Sanskrit reads as *bav*. Self-controlled and dignified, they slow down, withdrawing from outside activities and directing their prayers to eternity.

The Hindus never become enraged as they do not want to get upset (Michaux says), so if they want to sing, they sing. Those who want to pray, pray all day long. They trust animals like cows, elephants and monkeys, those sacred animals who resemble them. They appear peaceful and undisturbed by outside events, and by all means indifferent towards the outer world, which is nothing but illusion or *maya*. A cow, for instance, feeds by munching enormous quantities of grass, not clover really. Then it digests for hours everything it has swallowed.

I'm wondering whether I, a being that feeds on illusion, on the daily theater of barbarogenius, and on clover, I wonder if I will ever see the same thing there that Michaux saw? For everyone sees only that thing that they are supposed to see, some thing that they have already learned about a certain being or an object. Thus, they will see nothing more than what they have already seen or heard or have anticipated intuitively prior to a face-to-face encounter.

The Hindus, Michaux said, like the animals that do not ingratiate themselves to men, are drawn into deep meditation. They do not like cats and dogs for example because their character is too agitated and jittery…

The Hindus have to think over each and every action and we see them as such people in the early Indian films, way before Satyajit Ray's films came to town. In those early movies, the ferocious soldiers of a certain maharajah would take a couple of minutes to decide whether to get angry or not! Often in the end, they would be provoked and would get madly irrational. We can attest to this diasporic Indian "caricature" as it has been clearly shown since the turn of the 21st century in their dealings with the rest of the world. Today India counts for one of the leading countries that successfully got out of its economic recession, munching its own clover, grown in the freshest neoliberal soil.

As far as the animals go, a horse is far less interesting to the Hindu than, say, a camel. Camels rarely run and gallop, certainly less than a horse. It's a rather stable animal. The camel is known for its own tricks within the dromedary science, it places one hoof in front of the other, amused by its own slow pace. The Hindus respect slowness and stability, qualities reflected in their sense of the Hindi language. Hindi is slow and guttural consisting almost exclusively of consonants which trip over one another and then flow, heavy and crunchy. The highest religious hymns were composed in this language. Our European prayers and heritage appear almost ridiculous and vulgar when juxtaposed to theirs. Indian thought emerges from an occult background and is in essence crypto-magical. Moreover, it stays close to its oriental origins, a philosophy that always addresses the notion of the Supreme Being or Brahman. I am reminded of a jovial Michaux's observation that a Western philosopher loses his thin hair when he encounters a philosophical problem, whereas the "Orientals" let their hair grow while encountering the *aporia*. Their thoughts when addressing Brahman differ somewhat from our thoughts, so called European ones, as we are beings divided from the Absolute. As written in the Upanishads "Those who leave this world and have not encountered *Atman* and haven't got to know its essence, will not obtain liberation in ANY of the future worlds."

In order to reach that essence, the Hindus recite their mantras—and they breathe. One of the variations of the divine inhale-exhale technique is called *ujjayi*. A possible exercise could be: four inhalations through the left nostril, then you hold the breath, and then sixteen short exhalations through the right nostril. The prayer to the goddess of inhalation-exhalation, the goddess of creation and destruction, mother Kali, is ready to take off.

The Hindus believe more in the mother and the goddess of motherhood than they believe in the goddesses of femininity such as Radha, Lakshmi and Sarasvati, the sensual avatars of Shiva, their progenitor. If there is a notion of a saint with the Hindus, then it is the notion of mother as a symbol of sacrifice, a sacrificial symbol for the generations to come. They do not dwell in the past. The past is a living track, *akasha,* which constantly flows and manifests itself in the present moment. Mother is Big MA who entertains the order of all elements necessary for the sustenance of the species.

Equally true is that for the Hindu, the generation which follows is the one which counts because it prolongs the family and mankind and is thus more important than his own temporary (well)being. Sacrifice as a process is quite important. They have always sacrificed themselves for their traditions and their past, as much as they have sacrificed themselves to the modest moment they live in; sacrificing themselves even further for the generations to come. All the manifestations of the Asian Pantheon are sensual as they celebrate life and the Absolute in the most obvious way.

Compared to them, we Westerners look poor in our mourning for Christ, our absolute. In our churches and cathedrals we appear small and miserable, afraid in the darkness to face our Absolute.

They say a great ascetic, Ramakrishna, would get dressed in women's clothes because he yearned to be a woman loved by God, and then descend from his Pantheon in order to live with people. Hindu breviary is very practical as it prepares a being to fight the forces of evil in down-to-earth situations. The *Rigveda* is filled with concrete and practical advice about how to get on in life. There are mantras and offerings in the forms of incense, candles and food that help the believer attain the Absolute in a very practical manner. The concern here is not really with the decorative aesthetics of the offering. Much like in the most mystical form of Catholicism, a Hindu reaches the Absolute in his idolatry of ascetics and he prays in ecstasy. He adores the Absolute, makes prayers to him/her, does prostrations in front of his/her altars but he would never cry the way our Christian does: "*De profundis clamavi ad te, Domine!*" He will not yell and cry helplessly because a Hindu feels strong and powerful in front of his divinity. He is not a poor and helpless mouse in front of his own feeling of misery. He will force his God to help him. He will not tremble in front of him out of fear or cry out of sadness. He will sing out loudly and with an utmost *bav,* his AUM, and as soon as he has regained his calm he will gain force through his prayer, to spit at all the surrounding demons. He will not only threaten them like the Christians do, "get thee behind me Satan!" He will beat them down, destroy them morally and materially, so that Satan won't show up (at least in his head), for some good chunk of time.

And all this is happening rather slowly, in that slow yet at the same time sped up world of India. All of this is happening really slowly, as the Hindus never speed up. In fact, they never run.

His prayers are a chain of 38,000 verses of the Ramayana, up to 100,000 verses of the Mahabharata, all of which run slowly without any trace of epic (r) evolutions; no center of action, no peak, no poetic *denouement.*

All this Henri Michaux, Cartesian, recounted. Motivated, he counted all their verses in Sanskrit as far back as 1931 and now I wonder…

*****

What should we call, after all is said and done, a thought? Some poets say it is a unit of breath searching for its boundary, the brackets of its spirit (Atman). It is something that escapes us and flies away. This breath unit is divided in the West, but with the Hindu it is multiplied. The Hindu story of breathing has many legs, arms, subdivisions, and build-ups. This is how Gautama described all of this, an hour after he achieved his first enlightenment:

> The Sankaras stem from ignorance,
> our awareness comes from Sankaras,
> our name and form come from that awareness,
> the six realms arrive from the name and form,
> touch arrives from those six realms
> the feeling arises from the touch
> thirst arises from the feeling
> attachment follows from that thirst
> existence arises from attachment
> birth follows existence
> and then old age, death, sorrow, suffering,
> weakness, desperation follow, etc.

All schools of Buddhism agree in this: the main cause of *samsara* is pure attachment as it produces suffering (that of birth, of ageing, of sorrow, of death, etc.)

*****

Catherine and I arrive at the Paris airport under quite dramatic circumstances. We discovered at the last minute that the express train RER B, to the airport Charles de Gaulle, was not working that morning, so we were forced to take a taxi, which cost us a lot. In an airplane belonging to the Saudi Arabian company, destined to land in Riyadh, the air-hostesses clad in *chadors* hand us head phones and ear-plugs. We hear Hindi singers booming from all their 17 channels, but their choice of recordings is rather lamentable. I am quite positive that even last night I had a strange feeling, something like a foreboding, related to this whole trip, so I cried a lot—something I rarely do nowadays. I had a dinner with my son Vlad and friend Claude that very evening preceding the trip, and as the dinner was at the *Closerie des Lilas,* one of the best Parisian restaurants, that pleasant event was not the real reason I shed tears. All of a sudden I did not feel like going on that trip which, it seemed to me, had come like many other things in my life either too early or too late to enjoy its full impact.

I always wanted, so badly, to go on this particular trip with my first husband, Beau. But things in life took their own course and slowly but surely, the realization crystallized: our trip to India would never happen, never come true. I called him in London a few days ago and he said quite jovially "Oh, baby, call me from Kerala, if the need occurs—I could yell at those folks who annoy you in Hindi or Urdu if necessary, they will get it from me..."

Not only was Beau able, if I remember correctly, to speak fluently all the local languages, but as the son of a former Yugoslav ambassador on a mission to India and Pakistan, where Beau spent his youth, he was also well accustomed to their culture. And I always believed that that culture enveloped his entire being, like a luxurious oriental glove. He published his first book of poetry in Dhaka where he attended boarding school, but most of his poetry had been conceived in the local opium-houses of Sadarghat. Beau had never fully recovered from this "oriental" experience and has always felt terrible nostalgia for these regions which he left, but that often surf his memory. And so, this time I wondered if he simply would not, or truly could not join me on my trip. Perhaps if he did, the memories would be too painful.

I remember an old gentleman, Vlasta, "the Parisian" was his nickname, an old man from Paris who was born and grew up in my home town of Belgrade. Tito's communist regime had chased him out of his homeland and he had resided in Paris since 1945, where I and my visiting mother met him, circa 1990s.

My chatty mother asked him right away "But, sir, don't you wish to visit Belgrade again, just one more time, after 50 years? That's the town where you spent your most tender years."

"Oh, noooo!" exclaimed the old man. "Such a visit,

even the shortest one, would only kill me, I mean hurt me emotionally to the extreme for I would want to stay there. Not anywhere in that place. It has changed for me completely, and besides you never can go back to places which you left long ago. That's an illusion."

Perhaps the reason Beau lacked the desire to return to Pakistan lay in his words. However, I do not think that his refusal to travel was the reason I felt suddenly sad. Mine was a sentiment of great loss, a sentiment of being forlorn and lost to the challenges of youth, those challenges that we feel as young folks before the happy journeys which always start out mirthful and happy, and arrive to a happy end, as they were spontaneous, unpredictable and disorganized in their nomadic beauty. Now these were gone.

I got home late from the deluxe restaurant, paving my way through the sub stations of the Parisian metro and through the puddles of my own tears. I finally got home to the 18th arrondissement and found Chris's message to call him urgently before I set out for Kerala. When I called him in my teary voice to wish him Merry Christmas (as it was in fact December 23 already) he seemed to understand entirely my chagrin; he wanted to cheer me up, boost my energy.

Of course, who would understand me better than my poetry editor? These incredible, special, and non-commercial beings often professionally, but also on a private level, humanly and humanely interpret every single nuance of my words. And in fact we often talk of colors, certain thoughts of mine turned into words to be later printed on some good-quality paper. Out of all my past and future editors, my British editor was the most elegant and my most understanding interlocutor.

"Listen", he said, slightly worried on hearing my tears, "try to understand what it is that you need the most at this moment… And the state of mind you're in right this very second. I'd say that you need surroundings which are going to heal you, lift up your spirit and envelop it with some tender balm. Some place like the Ayurveda center *Keralayeem*, and that happens to be the place you're heading to anyways! But be careful there," he added, "be careful not to get ripped off by the local shamans and doctors over there as this is something that has just happened to a close friend of mine."

Oh, how much I cared for this Armenian once upon a time in this life time! When we met at London's St. Pancras train station, everything turned green and watery—in London the spring had just arrived! However little Tiki was with me at that time, banging his gong quite loud, announcing the end of our dreadful, already terminated relationship.

I stayed on Chris's boat on the Thames the entire month of May. That was just the beginning of a brilliant friendship, and an even more brilliant collaboration between a writer and her editor. And that relationship lasted and lasted—until one day its luster faded a bit and our friendship became a bit tarnished. Luckily, the dispute did not last for a very long time.

I feel that our dispute finally cleared out today and the sun has started shining again. The sun was, in fact, Chris/Aram's Armenian soul, not capable of staying serious and angry with me for very long. Do the Serbs and the Armenians have anything in common? Oh, yeah, they shared the same fear of the mighty Ottoman empire and their sultan. Yes, that was their common point just a century ago.

He told me once that his great-great grandfather, a doctor of the former Ottoman Sultan, once got a special order from the Sultan himself (this is all happening in Aleppo, unfortunate city in Syria where Chris/Aram happened to be born). The great-grandfather was to perform an emergency operation on the Sultan's nephew. The Sultan mentioned in passing that if his nephew did not survive the surgery he would kill all the Armenians in Aleppo! The great-great grandfather had performed this difficult task quite successfully. His trembling hand held the scalpel over the nephew's belly skillfully and the result was favorable for the nephew, and equally for the doctor. The Sultan was quite happy and he ordered that not only the Armenians be saved in Aleppo, but he gave large sums of *tallies* and *ducats* to the doctor. He also offered a generous grant of land, which the doctor did not want to accept. He took the gold and boarded a boat to Europe, more precisely in the direction of England where Chris's family remains to the present day.

IN THE MEANTIME

On board the Saudi airplane the hour of prayer has arrived. Everyone is falling on their knees ready to pray and pursue their evening prayer. There is a strange almost feudal feeling on the plane—for an instant it feels as if we are thrown back 200 years in history. Even the logo of the airplane company has an image of two prancing Arabian horses with sabers from Damascus crossed over their heads—these insignia make us believe we have found ourselves on some mad flying carpet and not on this powerful plane whose engine drinks tons and tons of the golden and black Arab kerosene. We should not forget (how could we?) that India, as much as Arabia, Persia and Turkey belong culturally, historically and politically to the part of the world that we conveniently call the Middle-East. These are, in fact, all countries made of roses. The houses are clad in roses, the suitcases painted pink. These are lands of warm, melted butter. The land's too sweet and too greasy and the air is filled with the utmost heat and trembles from it. The lands of the "hard and wild Arabic language," as qualified by Michaux. The lands of the ferocious Ottoman conquerors. But these are also lands of too heavy sweet perfumes, the lands of rose marmalade and *rahat-loukoums* made of rose. The Arabs have encrusted them into their architecture as we see in Spanish *Alcazar*, they built them into the gardens of

Alhambra where each and every detail is worked out and geometrically placed. There the *shadrvans* spurt their water with a certain economy, so much unlike their black oil which flows in abundance, and where their burning air slowly penetrates all their arabesques and flows through them and we cannot even imagine how this all happens.

There is the luxurious palace Taj Mahal in Agra, India, which is also a silent witness to Shah Jahan's love for his early departed Sultana. This grandiose building, built out of a huge and delicate chunk of marble, stands there trembling, a lump of white sugar. Juxtaposed to this building, our French cathedral of Notre Dame appears an old and somber tower, ruled by its gutters in the shape of medieval demons, whose towers invite their believers to jump off into the abyss of Christianity.

Although the Taj Mahal is endowed with numerous architectural elements, it floats in the air: its marble gate resembles a huge ocean wave which is snatched from the sea inadvertently; its whiteness seems illusory and weightless—it melts under the Mogul sun and merges with the aquatic silence of the Ganges. The Hindus enter this river in order to pray to the Absolute.

Michaux observed the fact that the Brits, despite their daily ritual of taking baths and showers, were detestable to the Hindus who did not appreciate their human qualities—they have always seen them as symbols of filth and moral baseness. The Hindus are incessantly bathing and applying perfumes to their bodies. Then they enter the Ganges, serious and determined. They rarely smile there, and they even brush their teeth in its water, as the teeth are an important source of a healthy life for them. They would not dream of swimming in it as this water is sacred to them, a center where ascetics lose their egos, their bodies resting passive in it. It is their magic ritual which allows them to forget their destitution, in the same space that they forget their hundred-percent hunger and their endemic cholera. The believers do not touch one another in the water, they are still divided into castes, as much as we, the so-called Europeans, though we pretend on our continent that the castes do not exist. As if they were not here, all around us, almost palpable. I say "we, the Europeans" never really believing we're anything like the "others" which did not altogether reflect Michaux's belief at the time he was writing, "A Barbarian in Asia".

In their book "Empire" Antonio Negri and Michael Hardt, big-time critics of Euro-centrism, talk about Moravia and Pasolini in the chapter "Two Italians in India." They basically discuss the different views of these authors in regards to India—Moravia was trying to fathom the differences between India and Italy, whereas Pier Paolo was trying to encompass their similarities. Neither of these two managed to overcome their initial sentiment of otherness, their feeling of Euro-centrism which kept them together in Italian literary history. And this feeling of belonging to Europe had evidently marked Michaux as well. Negri, whom I met in Paris a few days after he came out of prison, where he served time because of his political activism and his sympathy for the Red Brigades, thought that the only way to overcome Euro-centrism was to avoid accepting the norms which valued the cultural differences between Europe and India. Be it whatever it may be, in fact, I am ready to take my trip to India as if I were to travel to my local Indjija.

Italy, Serbia and India are not so different; at the same time they are just singular entities, as Deleuze would have explained when he was creating the notion of "singularity," opposing the notion of "otherness" which purported the Euro-centrist theory. In other words, one should view the cultural differences not so much as the post-effect of "otherness" but as an act of exhibiting equal cultural entities. What follows is a possibility of observing all cultural singularities as equal participants in our mutual presence, rather than treating them as different relics of the past.

Hey, it won't be so difficult for me to start this emancipatory procedure. Nehru, Tito and Nasser already started doing "it." Our distant neighbors, as well as those dwelling near us, have been equally modern, illuminated, and even as post-modern as we have been. They haven't been "more" or less developed than us, but they have been somewhat differently modern within the scope of their different modes of existence.

Everything I've been trying to say here escaped Michaux at the time he was writing his "Barbarian in Asia," as he was not really aware or conscious of these new modes of human co-existence. He told us his life-story, in which he traveled to Asia where he felt like a barbarian. He started feeling that the old, colonial division between us, "the Westerners" and them, "the barbarians" ceased to exist. Somehow, it was neither legitimate nor good, thus he came up with the self-ironic title for his travelogues. However, aside from irony, or self-irony, he could not go any further as he was endowed with his French heritage, the great inherited burden of his French culture, his European upbringing and education.

And this is how he saw the Asians at that point, he observed that "they are all tall and thin, without shoulders, without muscles, with square heads and frog's eyes whose gaze follows you wherever you go." Further on he says "their hair is beautiful though thick, soft and long, but their regard is somehow oily and as if covered with some thick film which usually resembles some oily trace left by certain cosmetic products; such a gaze follows you everywhere, however you do not feel inclined to look back at them." And further along he says "they are totally devoid of charm in their behavior, as if they were not alive, they are not too interesting to us."

Very well, my dear Michaux, if that's the way you saw them, and I know that perhaps all these peoples do not have our European sense of aesthetics, our "sense" of beauty, at work or in private, in their families. But they are endowed with the same feeling of the world that prevailed in "our" Byzantium, the sentiment which I call the "oriental Baroque." This feeling entails a vision that everything should be plentiful, too many elements are needed here, nothing should be sparse or lacking in substance or decoration. However, as this may appear to the ear of the 'sophisticated' westerner as too lofty a description for a certain kind of *modus vivendi*, I would like them to recall their paintings—that is, drawings and miniatures endowed with an acute sense of color and detail. Those paintings that speak of a specific refinement which in return has its own code and codex of existence, and its seductive effect on the eye of the beholder. I say "their" but this sentiment could be ours as well, if we were to freely enter the depth of their metaphysics, the core of their Absolute, and if we were to understand what inspires them to live and to exist, that knowledge would be ours and we would never feel in their lands as absolute foreigners.

The feeling of the Absolute

I remember Julia Kristeva once addressed me, turning her small orthodox eyes towards mine, in a moment which was for me rather heavy. "So, when and how did they bomb Belgrade?" she asked. And I remember clearly that she said "they" and not "we," although, perhaps, and according to Deleuze, it might have been that we did it, all of us! Perhaps if she were a French woman she would not have dared ask this question in such a direct and overwhelming fashion. This question I felt to be heavier and more lethal than any landmine as it was omniscient and overwhelming and included all people from our so-called Byzantium, where we could not return for a good while. However, this geopolitical turmoil in our Byzantium ended happily ever-after. Although as soon as it ended, it was quickly replaced, or sooner than later it would be replaced, with yet another new turmoil in Byzantium, as we have already witnessed, in the past. This appearance of the geopolitical replacement of turmoil in our lands we, the inhabitants of Byzantium, have already mastered in our respective kindergartens. Moreover, this situation had nothing to do with general linguistics, a science so dear and treasured in our regions. We have also understood that the geopolitical situations erupting eternally in the South of Europe, in the Mediterranean as well as in the Middle East, have always favored the science of ballistics over the science of statistics.

The airplane's music channel just happens to be emitting the mellifluous voice of the singer Lakshmiti Dohai Tomar.

She is a bit less sentimental than her Persian equivalent, lady Googoosh, who is in fact—to the great surprise of many of her fans—a singer of Ukrainian origin. However, both of thcm were less ferocious and wild than our own Ceca Raznjatovic… We are just flying over Riyadh, soon ready to land—and Dohai Tomar somehow prevents me from focusing on it.

RIYADH

A huge hexagonal capitol made of shiny, candy-flake marble, an ultra-wealthy capitol where the black liquid gold flows abundantly. It overflows, thus, all the Arabs smile at you with all the kindness and innocence with which wealth endows us—or could it be a smile of superiority? As if they haven't experienced any pain in their lives, in their history...

And the Bhagavad Gita[2] will tell us that there is more than one path which flows into the estuary of the spiritual river of human existence.

There is a path of action and meditation, thus the path of premeditated action, but also there a path of our intellect, as well as the path of pure heavenly divine love (bhakti). The goal of every path is to foresee the spiritual state in which an individual is going to find himself, in every situation, allegedly, he will feel the situation as an invisible part of himself. His state of being goes beyond that pain and suffering caused by the egoistic split which our being ("dasein") has produced in tearing itself apart from the outer world…

Michaux says that Europe has to look upon Asia—Europe has to lean on Asia's wisdom horizon, and this is something that the majority of the Hindus approve of as well.

---

2 *The Bhagavad Gita* often referred to as simply the Gita, is a 700-verse Hindu scripture in Sanskrit that is part of the Hindu epic *Mahabharata*

But, alas! Europe cannot lean on anyone else right now. Her time of holiday or a break, her era of peace and quiet is over. And what is Europe going to do now? It hasn't had enough time to rest, to recollect wisdom thoughts—it is tired and neurotic, lacking in freshness, going "off its rocker." Or as the popular joke goes: "Somewhat exhausted by her circumstances, a stupid, dumb, blonde, stopped for a second to ask her pal, a Joker from a circus named "The Deck of cards," "Joker, my dear friend Joker," she cried out—can you tell me how long exactly that "100 Years' War" between England and France lasted?"

The Joker had no answer.

Unlike the religious practice of Westerners, the Hindu prays alone and naked, in the depth of the darkest well of his quiet interior. He does it this way probably because he doesn't want anything, not even his clothes, to prevent his total union with the Absolute. He gathers that perhaps these clothes separate him from being one with the One. And when a Hindu makes love to his wife he thinks in fact of the Absolute, whose merest manifestation, the tiniest speckle of it, is embodied and epitomized in a girl's sensual body. At least, that's what Michaux said. I personally have never had the experience of making love to a Hindu. But then, Henri says, with a certain authority, that every living being should communicate with the Absolute including the animals. They should communicate with God as well, preferably in Temples, or in the areas designated for them to do so. Michaux quotes an incredible thing here: he attests to the presence of an infinite, almost suffocating love for everything spiritual over there. The Hindus seem to devour their divinity, and in every human aspect of their adulation they are Baroque. It is the utmost entropy of Baroque that one could find on this planet, they are the most legitimate children of Rococo, and beyond … For instance, when they utter the word "horse" the mere word does not suffice for them: they have to add "you know, that animal with four legs and four hooves, with a belly and an adequate saddle... or without an adequate saddle." Also, he emphasizes the fact that they are too stingy and frugal—a while ago they were the keepers of incredible wealth, luxurious booty, but today they are excellent, prudent accountants in every country where they happen to live. Give the managerial duties in a bank to a Hindu officer and he is likely to triple the profits. His sense of supreme spirituality has mingled with his supreme talent for the accounting.

In a sense, this nation has recovered its economy quite rapidly in the post-post-colonial period they've been facing. After the Brits left India, the Hindus inhabited one of the most populous and poorest countries in the world, the country which seemed to us, the Europeans, like a place not likely to recover soon. We thought the country would wallow in its poverty for a long time given the knowledge that Hindus are not rebellious people by character. It was not a part of their "religious system" to rebel, we thought, considering the politics of Gandhi. In 1919 the Brits massacred some 1500 helpless people who participated in Gandhi's peace march in Amritsar, Punjab.

It was only later that Jawaharlal Nehru, a Hindu born and raised in Kashmir, managed to successfully unite India, a country which definitively shook off the shackles of the British colonial power in 1947. He was sensitive to Moslem issues and a bit tougher than Gandhi. It seems that the aristocratic Nehru family, who gave India a bunch of lawyers, judges, barristers and solicitors, were quite strict when it came down to educating children. This straight education was perhaps due to their personal religion, or perhaps it had nothing to do with it. They say that Nehru himself, as the loving father of smart Indira, was a very meek and open-minded parent; and the way he treated his own children is the way he also treated his nation. He lived in a house surrounded by a sort of zoological garden in which the tigers, the monkeys and the birds all lived un-caged, unchained, at large—and in harmony. His zoo was the picture of Nehru's free India on a small scale. It is quite possible that his open-minded spirit inspired our comrade Tito (that is, in reality *his* comrade) who tried, on his own, on the Brijuni Island, to renew Nehru's Babylonian taste for gardening.

However, on the Brijuni one finds a different climate

set and different people from those in Delhi. The religion found on the Brijuni was different too. Christianity reigned over there, thus, given all the elements in that other garden, Tito's experiment turned rather into an unusual geopolitical caricature. Many political leaders from Western Europe, as well as representatives from his own country, reproached Tito his debonair and overly relaxed lifestyle in general, as much as the maintenance of the zoo garden in particular.

What is obvious for one culture does not go without saying for another, nor for their respective representatives. These two cultures—Tito's (Christian) and Nehru's (Muslim and Hindu), clashed in many ways. Nehru's Muslims and Hindus could not get along from the very start. Michaux had made a declamatory statement about this fact, using a metaphor which could only be rightly understood by botanists and zoologists:

When a snake spots a mongoose, he knows that their encounter will be a fatal and terminal one; as for the mongoose—he is not bothered by such an encounter and he does not even think about the fact that the snake may not or may like him. Deeply despising him from the start, the mongoose just stares at the snake preparing to crush it, in the next second he is not even thinking about his new tasty mouthful.

The Turks, the Afghani, the Persians, the Ethiopians and the Malayans have all endured the influence of the Arabs and the influence of Mahomet. The Arabs might appear angry and, according to Michaux, their religion appears menacing. He remembered that ancient "There is only one God, and Mohammad is his prophet," the only prophet with the sword, some people would add. And these people started fearing Islam. This fact was heavily negated by the most intelligent of my ex-husbands, a Persian prince and the last of inheritors of the Qajar dynasty. He claimed that the sword has only symbolic function and that its place in the Holy Scriptures serves merely as a reminder—in the Koran, for instance, as a psychoanalytic symptom of a certain Lacanian orientation. As a grandson of the most illustrious sultana, Mahd Olia (Malek-Djahan Khanom), and a descendant of the ancient dynasty which was replaced violently by the Pahlavi, my ex had duly studied his Shiite heritage, it being a spiritual, more metaphysical version of Islam. He concluded that the terrorist formations, above all ISIS, have erroneously interpreted the Holy Scriptures, which have never, and will never, propagate or advocate violence above over or towards (the Big) Other.

True, Michaux remarked, an Arab would greet you often with the following: "Let good health and fortune meet one who follows the *true* religion!" He adds, a bit maliciously, that this may mean that good health and fortune should not serve those who do not follow (that) religion.

The real Arabic character is reflected in a desert—it is infinite, pure, without flowers or images, or any surrounding decorations. The Arabic God's vision is "pure" and as such tends to aspire towards the absolute. Everyone bows to such a God, throwing themselves into the sand or onto the prayer rug in a mosque. He is honored loudly. Their language is somewhat rough, explicit, full of consonants, with a hard "h" that drove the French like Michaux crazy, because the French language does not recognize the letter "h" in its pronunciation. And in this particular letter we find a secret lever of the colonial practice, even nowadays. If you remove the letter "h" from an Arabic word, a member of this linguistic group may feel rather castrated; it is as if you neglected a greater part of their history and tradition. Aware of this phenomenon, I tend to correct my students at la Sorbonne every time we start a class, during the first five minutes that I take their attendance and call their names. I am trying to avoid all racial, psychological, traumatic and linguistic misunderstandings while remembering the bright examples of enlightened teachers such as Adam Mickiewicz:

You are not Asan, but Hasan. Please pronounce your name correctly, because if you do not say it correctly no one else will pronounce it correctly for you.

My words often appear to them as a magic formula, and by the time they manage to retrieve some of their lost national dignity—which had been utterly shaken in front of the French authorities—the students start feeling love and sympathy towards me—at any rate, they have never heard these words at la Sorbonne before.

And then Michaux says—and here I completely agree with him—that the entire Arabic alphabet is in a form of an arrow which hurls towards the sky, and that it could be seen in only one letter, one sign which, somewhat like in Hebrew or in a Chinese pictograph, represents a curve, a decorative path of one line which consists then of many short, tiny lines gliding from the left onto the right side. Such letters, when they are inscribed on a paper, are four times faster to read than our "western" alphabets. The Turks have allegedly barely got used to our slow writing, once they accepted our Latin alphabet in their schools. They say their communication slowed down after they adopted our modes of writing. Arabic is a fast language of warriors—there it resembles Latin in this respect: it is full of short and just words filled with the tonic, sonorous and stressed bravado which form lapidary and fast sentences. It is a brave language, knightly and *chevaleresque*, and as such it still somewhat belongs to the Middle Ages. And as such, it differs greatly from Hindi spoken by the Hindus who did not appropriate Muslim religion. Michaux had pertinently noticed that while watching the Hindu temples, one could also recognize the qualities inherent in their language—they are open spaces. The Arabic is fast as if it was conceived for quick prayers in a mosque whose interior is clean and empty resembling, according to Michaux, a "colored jail." The Hindus had lost their independence though, eight centuries ago, after the conquest of Alexander the Great (here we have the art of Gandhara to attest to his conquest). Then they watched some other Greek rulers pass through their land, then the Moguls, the Huns, the Brits and some other lesser-known conquerors who also left traces on this immense empire. Michaux says the Hindus resemble the elephants—animals who are good-natured but sometimes cruel. As they remember all the details of an interaction, they can also get mad and trample everyone and everything with their mighty feet, just at the moment when we think that we have completely mastered their behavior and made them our friends.

****

I have just stepped into the toilet at the airport in Riyadh, set in marble. I want to change there. My clothes from Paris are too warm for this climate. And culturally these clothes don't fit this land in which all women sit under a veil. They are made-up Salomes who wear jeans and patent leather high-heel shoes under their long veils and chadors. So I am in a toilet set in marble which is at the same time a bathroom and a hammam with a *shadirvan* (fountain), when four women under burkas start to knock at my toilet's door. They hide under these burkas two infants each, but I hear their voices in English:

"Hurry up, please! Madam, you can change outside of the toilet too."

I'm coming out of the toilet furious, ready to take on one of those imperial, and also, imperialistic postures. We learned this kind of speech in the communist regime where only some yelling from the "above" upper hand was enough to establish some sort of peace, ephemeral as it appears today.

"Oh, c'mon! You should be ashamed of yourselves! Here is your Valide Sultan, a daughter-in-law of the grandson of the great Nasser-Edin Shah, visiting here her lost provinces and regions. You should respect her, not bang at her door like this..."

Awed, they glanced at me and stepped back. All four of them spoke at the same time:

"Selaam Aleikum, Great Sultana, we are so sorry, Madam! Hamduliallah!"

They were so modest and quiet all of a sudden, they resembled the women from Bosnia with whom my mother grew up, long before she quit Bosnia. I let them enter the room full of turquoise mosaics. They had to change young children and infants, both of us, them and me, pressed down with centuries of oppression.

In their Arabic there were no vowels, the "evil" fruit of leisure which all the speakers of Arabic swallow up as they are ashamed of them, thus everyone always hears a platoon of fast consonants just as I hear them now. These women were truly in a hurry to catch a plane. God knows where to.

A part of my spiritual path, *ahimsa*, was to protect them; a part of me really wanted to leave this place, but I felt a deep urge to know something—who I really was and where I was coming from (as if these women could only explain these facts to me!!). I expected, or at least a part of me did, to dream karmic dreams the following days and nights and that all the explanations, answers to my questions, would come to me in dreams. I was in a hurry to get to Kerala, to the very south of India, and my heart was covered by some sad power of insecurity.

It was not that I desired or had a need for anything at that moment: I witnessed the death of every desire and emotion. The woman who was a companion on this trip, all of a sudden, appeared quite young to me, she looked like a child who hadn't lived a quarter of a century. She was steadily turning around herself, like an idiot, while asking me short, irritable and irritating questions, extremely happy that we would get to Kerala the very next day and start doing our YOGA—as if the yoga we were doing was not a certain inner discipline which required no school or mat for the physical prostrations we were about to do. If you received certain yoga instructions once, it would either reflect onto your soul like those multiple cascades from the *shadirvans* mirroring your knowledge, or you would forget it immediately. The same way Michaux forgot the alphabet and turned it into drawings. René Daumal understanding everything, yoga's quintessence, went on to write his "Rasa," or "taste" in Sanskrit—which somewhat reflects the quintessential quality of our truc nature.

****

I have been walking for hours along these endless marbled corridors of the airport in Riyadh—the prayer rugs cover each and every corner of the freshly built-up halls—many of which seem to be patched up and put together quickly and lavishly: here is a stand for a 1001 variations of Haagen-Dazs ice-cream, and there, just next to it, is a stand selling Ramadan's white *halva*. Would they sell, in their Duty Free, that white halva with pistachios or the one with almonds?

No, no and no. I tell the vendor that I would like to buy a box of rolls with walnuts, or the so called *gurabia* cookies, to which he benevolently nods his head and asks: "You mean the gazelle's corns?" Yes, it is the same thing in Libya and Lebanon—where they call that cake from finely cut dough "angel's hair" or *yahabibi*, and in Serbia or in Turkey they call it *kadaïf*... I will taste none of these cakes obviously, as the aggressive representatives of air companies have started announcing our flight to Cochin. All of a sudden, an incredible stampede of people of all colors—black, blue and white—starts, as all of them want to get in line for the overcrowded flight. Oddly enough, this stampede does not bother me and I find it highly amusing: wrapped in my light green scarf I smile to the crowd surrounding me. I exclaim "Selam Aleykum" and "Aleykum selaam" to people around me and after these niceties they all let me go ahead towards the ramp leading to the plane. When I tell Catherine that everyone would be much nicer to her if she also addressed them nicely with their "Bonjour" that is, with "Selam Aleykum," she looks at me relieved and flabbergasted, as if I told her how to obtain hot water in the far North Pole.

So there we are, already on a plane which is awfully crowded and hot—the air conditioner's broken, there are babies (perhaps some fifty of them altogether) and they all cry loudly, forlorn, a lost chorus in this humid and suffocating situation. I close my eyes in the center of this chorus and for a second I fall asleep, float away, as if I am Sarasvati, the goddess of poetry, noise and music in person, I nicely float away.

The Indians often see their children as their karmic parents—they often call babies their "father" or "mother" and often they pray to them, to their whole family who are their own Pantheon. They have composed many hymns and songs to honor them and even their most avant-garde interpreters include them in their repertoire—Sheila Chandra and Anoushka Shankar are the post-modern girls whose entire musical heritage is based on the religious hymns from their traditional Hindu repertoire.

COCHIN, end of December, noon

Our suitcases have arrived and we arrive after them. It had taken an awfully long time, the passport check and filling out health regulation forms, (are you coming from an area afflicted by Ebola, or Yellow fever?, etc.). We are greeted by a charming "Zen Tours" driver who takes us to the city. There, in an unknown hotel, we are supposed to meet with the rest of our small French group of yoga teachers and trainees our organizer and yoga instructor Renan and, finally, eat lunch. Cochin ili Kochi (the pronunciation of this word depends on the origin of the speaker) is a city which consists of many huge trees, of quickly built suburbs that Americans call shanty towns. However, these new "burbs" emerge somewhat directly from lush and generous Indian forests. There is poverty and misery here, present and palpable, however, they are embedded into this lush countryside, and like a nail grown into one's finger, and these parts are not to be considered, in terms of urban development, separate from their balmy green background. This sort of "urban" scenery I'd already observed in West Africa—the fire trees, Jacaranda trees, coconut palms and banana trees—all of them so different from the dusty towns where we usually reside. The landscape here reminds me terribly of the West African bush in Northern Nigeria, on the Sahara border, near the city of Kaduna where Beau and I lived some thirty years ago. That time evaporated somehow, but memories are solid and they stand erected over the uneven hills of our melancholy years. Anyways, this sort of humid, subtropical climate is the natural breeder of this lush greenery.

The weather is terribly humid and hot around here. I take two different anti-mosquito sprays from my suitcase—I carried them all the way from Paris, along with some pills against paludism (malaria) which I have to take for a month so that they work. If I missed one, my daily dose, they would have no effect, my French doctor told me. Now I remember clearly how my romantic episode got interrupted in Nigeria, which is my African life with Beau—I got malaria at one point, and it's a terrible disease where you shake with the bed you're lying in, and all the covers are constantly wet from your cold sweat and the fever goes on and on and on...

However, here we are now in the hotel of "healthy living" and organic, fresh foods, with a tiny group of those hunters for the vitamin-enhanced cells which soften wrinkles—they are seated at a large oblong table waiting for lunch. How did they get over here I wonder... how and, oh good Lord Shiva, why? They probably had some inner, hidden motive which propelled them to come here; and that might have been their need to adore something or someone. They have heard about the Hindus and their innate love for magic acts and rituals.

I think Michaux could help us with his explanation when he said that the Hindus like to venerate other beings as much as they expect these venerated beings to become their followers. Or they might have felt a need to venerate objects, the receptacles of love and adoration like that particular bride who did not wear the necklace given to her by her bridegroom, but placed that precious object on a coconut. The coconut was different from her neck though; it was carved and made to be an object of common adoration. So now we had a woman who adored not only her husband, the necklace and the coconut, but she also had friends, a sort of team of people who were supposed to adore her necklace, the coconut and, perhaps her own husband—however, we are not so sure that the husband wanted to be so much adored and venerated by her entourage. The objects of adoration can be different, it could be anyone or anything, and just as an agriculturist adores his plow and his coach, it does not imply that he adores them religiously. However, he would bow over them, his body taking on a reverent form of the object he "adores," until his body soon acquires the shape of the object he adores. Michaux noticed that the Hindus adore both people and objects—this is because

1. They like rituals (allegedly, they breathe in and breathe out 7 times before they utter a single word).

2. Because they like to deepen any given situation and to add a certain weight and importance to it. They do it even in a situation when they are in a position to give a simple "yes" to something. In fact they say "yes,"

but not in a way we do, by nodding our heads, they drop their heads left and right, as if the head was suspended on some magical see-saw. Even if you told them that they would be offered 1,000,000 dollars, they would not react to your words by saying "yes, thank you," but rather start wiggling their neck and turning their head from left to right as if they were proud swans who just stretch their long necks. But what the Hindus really believe in is the attitude of non-violence. Gandhi did not have to try hard in order to inspire his people in that direction, they were already for him, in other words, the seed of non-violent attitude has lived with them for centuries.

First of all—there was the founder of Jainism, which is one of the most important religions in India—who ordered the Hindus not to eat after sunset as he dreaded a possibility that an insect might fall into his soup and he might even swallow it. By mistake, of course, but Jainism forbids people to hurt insects.

Then, there was Buddha, the sad prince Gautama who decided to keep his smile on so that he would not cry all the time "in the face of so much misery in the world." Buddha offered his body to the tigress, as he was sorry to see her that hungry and famished. On Buddhist *tankas* we often see this image of a tigress surrounded by baby tigers who are waiting in turn for their piece of the meal, after mom has finished with the major part of Buddha's body.

Hinduism, as a religion, respects both monotheism

and polytheism, animism, pantheism as well as all sorts of demonic cults. The well-off and the successful would adore Brahma, but those coming from the lower caste would be allowed to venerate only Kali, Shiva and their numerous avatars.

(the camera-angle moves to) :

HOTEL JACARANDA

The Jacaranda Hotel is entirely surrounded by lush jacaranda trees in full bloom. It is the end of December, and the clock has barely reached noon, but the temperature outside has already risen to 35 C degrees. A few dogs and a kitten sleep in a lazy slumber in the sunny courtyard which leads to the hotel's entrance. It's a small but comfortable deluxe hotel with salons all decorated in the "British colonial style"; right to the left of the entrance there is a large dining room which presently houses a huge, lavishly decorated "Swedish buffet." In fact, the Swedish buffet consists exclusively of Indian and Pakistani spicy pastries and some sweet and sour (mango chutney) spreads. An elderly matron with fancy sunglasses, who has studied Buddhism with the monks residing in Paris, is eager to know what I really mean by presenting myself and saying "hello" to her. Let us call her "Michelle." So, I ask Michelle which school of Buddhism she belongs to.

"What school? But I am not going to any school," she quickly responds, throwing back in disapproval, her stupid, huge head. The rest of the group consists of some rich and forlorn younger women, who visit certain Indian or Indonesian *ashrams* up to fifteen times a year in search of enlightenment—they almost all look alike.

All of them except for a younger girl with silicone lips who somewhat appears lost in this company. She does not resemble the rest of this party, so I take liberty to remind her to take off her jewelry and store it aside as such demonstration of expensive private property may provoke danger to her personal security. The locals are all under the poverty level, at least according to our "western" standards, thus someone who wears a diamond necklace may invoke something other than admiration. At least, I can speak for myself; my experience of the third world also taught me to worry about things like that.

She throws an amiable, modest look of recognition and gratitude in my direction, and then she asks where I am from. And what did I think about this group of our fellow-travelers. Did they seem like cool and nice people to me? What could I say to her? Nothing. Silence and contemplation could be real ornaments, real gems too, sometimes more valuable than those encrusted into some pricey necklace. She told me her name was Shirin and that she did not come over here just "to do yoga," but above all, to see this vast phenomenon called India. Here is the first intelligent observation that anyone has made in front of me after these long two days of our non-interrupted voyage. I tell her yoga's not bad, after all there are several types of yoga, and the physical manifestation of an otherwise spiritual discipline is also called yoga. However "we", the Westerners, don't see "yoga" in sports gyms in Europe as a continuation of a much more cryptic tradition which is the basis of the real Hindu yoga.

I said I liked her open-minded attitude which was her desire to see India, the country, and its vast civilization and then I promised to join her the following day on her visit to the temples and the city which was located near our recreation center. At this point, our charming teacher and organizer, Renan de Germain arrives in the hotel, his presence interrupting all other conversation. De Germain was a descendant from an old French aristocracy, the fact which we would have guessed right away, whether he ever mentioned his origins or not. He casually walked into the hotel as if it had already belonged to him in the past. He immediately started recounting his numerous adventures, from those in Bombay (Mumbai), where he stayed for a couple of days prior to our arrival, to more recent ones—his trip from the airport of Cochin to the Jacaranda Hotel, among others. Bombay was an ideal place for him where he spent numerous nights attending "crazy parties" which were "exactly like the parties he frequented in the Marais in Paris." He announced his intention to move to the city as soon as we finished our yoga workshop in Kerala. Bombay was for him "the capitol" of every action, it was the center of the entertainment industry in India where Bollywood productions had already acquired an enormous reputation... Renan was accompanied by a light-headed millionaire woman, named Lily, who would every couple of minutes burst into desperate bouts of laughter, which, sadly enough, resembled a hyena's laughter more than anything else.

Now we are about to head out for the Ayurveda center, the Keralayeem, which is some good two hours away from Cochin by a local bus. The heat becomes unbearable, overbearing with humidity, which like a fine moist foil, envelopes all the coconut leaves, the palm trees, the lianas and the quickly-built houses in the tawdry parts of town that we've been passing through.

KERALAYEEM

This center is a god's gift, and the very look of it causes your *ujjayi* to stop for a split second. However, it is situated at the banks of a lake which, covered like it is with thick layers of fog exuding humidity—well, it looks more like an unhealthy and ugly marsh than any romantic house of well-being. This large conglomerate of big cabin houses and tiny buildings made of straw was interspersed with numerous channels in this quasi paradisaical and picturesque setting filled with numerous plants and herbal species. There were also those tiny boats, which float down the river all lit up like Christmas trees. But above all, this setting is populated with tiny bungalows which coast in the midst of all that vegetation…

In fact, as I'm writing this, it's five o clock in the morning and I'm on the veranda of a bungalow where I was placed with another... hmm, say lady, and all around I can hear the twitters and cries of the most unusual feathers, having merged their birds' voices into a wild cacophonous morning operetta. I simply can't fall asleep. However, my insomnia does not come either from the fact that I got excited arriving to an utterly foreign civilization, or from the fact I've been munching this strange poisonous medication whose effect is rather severe on my sinuses and my lungs. My insomnia comes right from discomfort at being thrown into the bungalow at the edge of the Indian bush with a totally incompatible traveling companion. She's an elder dominant lesbian, with hard and menacing looks. In other words—a woman who has always striven to become a man, something she succeeded in becoming, even if only partially.

She used to work as an accountant for a big corporation and today she is a retired researcher, a student of Sanskrit at Paris University, who snores loudly so that even the smallest idea of falling asleep seems ludicrous to me. I'll have to try hard to transfer myself to another bungalow this morning, long before our five-hour *vinyasa yoga* class begins. It goes on without breaks and ends in a one-hour meditation, which serves, according to the collective experience, as a sort of remedy against any sensation of heat, any headache, any feeling of hunger. After meditation, we don't even feel being invaded by the mosquitoes which continue to buzz around, in chords, all over this humid marsh. They say this is truly the land of malaria and its real kingdom—and the natural habitat of the mosquitoes.

Alright, I will sink into my own meditation, a short *samadhi* (an absolute spiritual calm), whatever that may appear to be, right now, this very morning, three days before the celebration of the New Year in Europe where I resided and longed to escape, if just for a minute.

Interesting, Michaux remarks, for the Hindu, the

act of natural meditation is almost equal to an act of sexual unification. He thus thinks that they often meditate in the open, that is, that they pursue that path of open physical encounter, free, unbound sexual act which appears as a totally natural activity. On top of everything, natural as it is, this activity has been found on numerous representations, and on numberless reliefs of all their big temples. And Michaux remarked: "Not even the Kama Sutra appears to be a book a Hindu would hide under his table while reading it, hidden from family." Here he quotes the names of numerous temples with ornate reliefs which contain the images of sexual acts or the images of various sexual positions "which would be comprehensible even to a young child" as they are that clear and explicit. However, all their sexual acts are sacred as their execution has only one unique goal: the union of a man with the Absolute. During his entire sexual encounter with the Other, a Hindu dreams and fantasizes about one thing—becoming one with God. The sexual act devoid of such unification with God does not lead to anything valuable, it is a "worthless word" and an infection of our soul, a mere mirage, a seduction of flesh and appearance, as it is a vain movement of absurd gestures, those of our bones and transpired sweat.

They live in unity with their sexual organ which serves them as the center of their daily, or better—their eternal stability! However, they don't even notice it as for them it is not an organ of sexual desire and/or daily lust—it is there for them as part of their daily decorum, exactly as in the ancient theatre, *Kalidasa,* where characters discuss the secrets of love and love-making in a non-erotic, almost anatomical manner. A young girl asks herself "don't I feel that liquid oozing out of my vagina, that ointment which precedes the act of love?" And then she adds: "I'd better shut up—so that no one can see what's deeply hidden in my heart." Michaux believed every European would have been ashamed while reading this play—perhaps it was only he who felt ashamed in that forgotten year, 1931, when he was living out his role of a French Surrealist in India?

However, it is true even today the representatives of the Hexagon, as well as the rest of the international neo-liberal mafia, they take love to be an impermanent, temporary expression of a powerful sexual attraction, and the Hindus look at it as a stable constant at the bottom of a long and tall ladder which takes us to the Absolute. I wonder if my so-called "trip to India" is a sort of journey that is at the same time the deepest and longest journey to the heart of our interior. I mean the interior of a person, that rarely found person who fathoms the truth that Monotheism is a form of violence, that this religious system is a dictatorship of the Absolute over humans. Here the image of the Absolute is closer to that of the pimp who keeps those poor Ukrainian girls locked in a room of a seedy Parisian hotel, while feeding them opiates (as Marx pertinently remarked: religion=opium for people). He (the "Absolute") has to do that so the girls (people) keep quiet, so they don't wake from their existential slumber and rebel against his exploitation. The Hindus, even when they believe in only one deity, invite us to pray to ALL other deities, collectively, as we are doing just now, sitting in the position resembling a lotus flower.

We need a special path to reach the Christian God, a special ladder made of rules and regulations, whereas the Hindu deities are omnipresent, all around us, as their believers maintain, they manifest in all their natural and unnatural forms and in their magic and ordinary aspects. Today in fact, a Hindu would not kill anyone in order to please his Absolute (I will double check my statement as I look into the altars of secret societies in their temples); however, I am sure his angel or assistant does not carry a sword or a nuclear rocket on him. It seems the Hindu would like to live in peace with the whole world, today, as ever. Ninety -five percent of their population does not eat meat, although, ok, we do know that being a vegetarian does not automatically imply goodness and the peaceful intentions of a character.

Here we have four phases in the development of their spiritual universe:

Brachmacharya is the first step, adolescence filled with virtues such as obedience, innocence.

Grihasta is the phase when one lives within his community, an individual gets married and his social life flourishes.

Vanaprastha is a period of subsequent departure from community and social life.

Sannyasa is the last phase in the lifetime of a spiritual being, the phase when he relinquishes a secular life style.

The major obstacles on this noble path of realizing oneself and the Absolute are ignorance and sexual curiosity, which the Hindus consider to be different from the natural, nurturing love that a man gives to a woman or to his family. One of the major obstacles here is basic curiosity we show towards the world and its events—a quality which informs a larger geography of the human spirit.

I'm afraid here, that my entire life path, heavily sprinkled with curiosity—according to their belief—has been a pure failure. My life path, oh yes, has been burdened with obstacles I have been surmounting more or less successfully, until the moment I reached this holy place, Keralayeem!

I've just been reading an article which says that the Hindu gods behave similarly to our western heroes (Greek heroes, heroes from the Middle-ages, etc.), or as ordinary people who hate violence and try to prevent it. They are people, in fact, but people with special magical powers. The locals do not see them as dignified saints, but rather as people with incredible, higher powers.

According to the legend, Shiva, the supreme deity, had four wives, Parvati (Sati or Dakshayani), Uma, Durga and Kali, but he would make love most of the time with the first lady, the epitome of charm and romantic endeavor. While the two of them were having fun Vishnu and Brahma came to visit, and to their great surprise, found that Shiva would not interrupt his divine love-job for their visit. So, these two sat down and waited for Shiva to show, but after a while they left to mind their own business. A little later, Shiva stopped his divine activities and looked around, wondering what had happened there in his absence. He then touched his penis and exclaimed "oh, friends! This penis also signifies Shiva, as much as his hand does or his very arm and legs. And people who respect this stupid penis of mine I will respect and venerate as much as they venerate me."

These wise words were coined by an ancient, several thousand-year-old civilization. Although its society is still divided into castes (and which one isn't?), it allowed all its citizens to live under its given circumstances in the most acceptable way, not refusing itself any pleasure in life. The veneration of their deities is the force which keeps this community together, as they pray together and celebrate a divinity which is nothing other than a form of communal living aspiring to their supreme Brahma. As far as the *chandalas* go, they are still, in this 21st century treated as beings coming out of every caste. The real puss and cancer on the face of India are the Dalits or the "untouchables" who haven't succeeded up to the present day to integrate into the Indian social system, where they would obtain basic human rights.

Vivekananda was their guru or saint who tried to unify all the castes and religions, creating a theosophical system capable of improving their entire society. However, in India, the Hindus have always prayed to their different deities, especially in the South and in Sri Lanka; the Muslims have always said that "there's no God but.. and Mohammad is his prophet," and the Christians were those white folks who reached this country as the missionaries or the conquerors, depending on how one takes it. Vasco da Gama, the founder of the first Catholic church in Cochin had brought the Lord's servants to Kerala who went around reading their Gospel, at the same time, trying to convert the Muslims and the Hindus to "Christ's thing."

However, the white man has learned something in this region as well—the millions of those who have always wanted to penetrate the secrets of this land—they came and went, and they are still coming over in great numbers as the latest fashions have dictated: they have to learn how to not eat meat, to sit in the posture of the supreme meditation, to not criticize everything and everyone that moves around them. They have to learn how to get rid of the defensive attitude that flies out of their mouths every time they try to breathe. They learn here how to breathe, how to fast, how to inhale and how to exhale empty air, how to make use of their lungs instead of tending always to their stomachs, which are not going to accept meat any longer, etc.

We, the Westerners, always get confused while receiving the first meditation instructions: how are we going to inhale the air which we believe we have always breathed in and out? This pure air escapes us, it is faceless, spreading in all directions, it does not belong to anyone in particular; it is innocent and birth-less; it is the most intimate part of our intake as it feeds us and at the same time does not mess with our senses. As we breathe, we become aware of the senses again. Breathing the air in is not a very heavy job, but to push that air into our abdomen and into other parts of body, into the midst of our frontal area where the white light resides—is quite a big job. We wash our thoughts in this light so that all thoughts become one, and then that one ceases to be important as it further enters the region where all thinking disappears. If one ignores or slights the quality of this Hindu thought, whitened by light, which is in fact a shortcut to the understanding of the Hindu philosophy, he is bound to commit an error—as explained to us by a contemporary philosopher Slavoj Žižek, who conversed about this with a French thinker, Fabien Tarby.

In this conversation though, Žižek expressed several radical opinions—he called Gandhi "a soft fascist" because Gandhi had "just sympathized" with the caste of "untouchables"—without any real effort on his part to abolish that caste. Indeed, arrogant as any other Western thinker in the age of neocolonialism, Žižek says Gandhi tried to bring every caste its proper dignity, but failed to abolish them altogether. Žižek wonders why Gandhi couldn't, or wouldn't do that for India.

Gandhi's society had witnessed the massacre of thousands of innocent Indians in Amritsar when the population, on a peace march, did not show any resistance to the British colonialist cannons in 1919. When we speak about the mentality of a certain nation or that of an entire civilization, we have it here, and Gandhi was probably deeply aware of the fact that 20th century India was not France in its revolutionary glory, nor did he see himself as the Indian Danton or Robespierre of his time. And he probably did not think the masses would follow the revolutionary, armed hero Ambedkar, who was in favor of an armed putsch—an action similar to the armed conflict proposed by the ultra-left wing Marxists in Latin America in the wake of the 21st century.

True, Žižek has encountered such a revolutionary figure, but in the body of a taxi driver during the thinker's semi-official visit to New Delhi. Allegedly, the driver hugged the philosopher after a cordial exchange of heavy jokes between them during their ride. Žižek quotes the driver here who asked him if he knew "why Gandhi used to walk naked with his proverbial cane through the Indian villages", to which the philosopher replied "the historical peace fighter probably looked for some sturdy guys who would place that cane in the right place."

All things are possible, and probably this meeting between taxi driver and Žižek really took place. It is also possible a Slovenian philosopher and the Indian driver really became "brothers".

In an earlier page in this book I recorded Michaux's remark about that old Indian legend that tells a story about Shiva and his consort, and the moral being to advise us to see the Hindu more like ordinary people and less like Gods and deities: above all, they are people who possess an animistic belief in all that is human and humane in their Gods and in nature, so I don't see a problem here. We can see their Gandhi as a hero, a demi-God who changed the course of their history, but we could also see him as a simple, ordinary man who sought pleasure in life. Or rather he tried to defeat that sense of pleasure in himself, or was asking for too much of it—by seeking utmost asceticism (if we interpret Lacan/ Žižek *stricto senso* here). The hardest thing of all is to interpret Gandhi as a "soft fascist" and here we need not listen to the Žižekian interpretation of Lacan in order to fathom the famished figure of Mahatma Gandhi. And if we advance in reading our Žižek here, we are bound to ask ourselves whether his profoundly Eurocentric vision was large enough to accommodate the philosophical system of the Far East, which tends to be, above all, theosophical from its very beginning to *ad infinitum*...

And finally, one of the nicest thoughts about Gandhi comes from Henri Michaux, who urges us to read *Hind*

Swaraj or the book on *Indian Domestic Rules*; he suggests we read this one and then right after a book by any Western philosopher or sociologist. The French writer says we would notice a great difference between the authors, but that our compliments would go to Gandhi. His book is filled with love towards ordinary people... it is not a "holy" book by any means, but is noble in spirit—Gandhi though, as a young man used to be "a maniac of reasoning," as he was a lawyer first then a peace fighter. Anyway, the absence of the so-called egoist's approach to others became truly proverbial. Some people considered him fairly naive when he declared that he would not mind having the British stay in India, only if they became peaceful and loving towards Indians and if they would finally stop killing cows and bulls. Michaux really did not believe the Brits were capable of renouncing their legendary steak, not for anyone in this world, let alone the happiness of some other nation. He also nicely remarked that Gandhi's own people started to love less their leader because they started reading extensively "our Western books, as they study at our universities." European civilization is a very specific religion no one can resist, said the French poet as early as 1930.

Žižek claims yet another thing concerning Christianity. He says "only Christianity tore the shroud of religion and entered freely into philosophy, as it was the only (religion) to promise the creation of some new, egalitarian community." Under the shroud of our agitated history we can hear his words (but we really don't have to) as some musical, symphonic truth.

What he mentions also, in his meditation on the Far East, is the fact that when a lady wears a burka, the supreme veil covering her entire face and body, it does not imply her refusal to engage socially. And he asks that we should question ourselves about what the uncovered face of the Other could mean to us? If we imagine that the Other could be someone monstrous and inhuman, his face is just a reflecting screen, sort of refusing the possibility of Real contact with another person. "Here I see you, you see me, you're smiling at me, you appear sweet to me." All of this could be a mirage, a trap, a charade offered to us by a highly visible, uncovered face.

Thus, the Slovenian thinker says, a patient does not look into the analyst's face while in session, recounting his/her personal story. The analyst won't discover his story by looking at the patient's face. He may even discover some profound lie, like in the case of Salomé who, after taking off all her veils, was still begged by Herod to take off something more. And what was she to remove—her own skin? So, do we see how wearing a burka reflects this approach to reality?

The burka reveals rather than conceals the face of the Other. When we tear the face, skin on the face, we see the real brutality of the other, and that imaginary illusion that the naked face offers.

Michaux though, in his travelogue, admires the modesty of the young Bengali girls and women who cover their faces quietly as soon as a stranger crosses their path. They even cross the street or move to the far side of the pavement when a stranger approaches. Michaux appreciated their attitude and found them incredibly charming, unlike the English ladies whom he found too naked "offering themselves blatantly," which got on his nerves. "They walk this world totally naked so any mangy dog can touch their legs; or they don't cover their face or lower their gaze; they bare their breasts and they are ready, waiting for someone to jump on them".

WHILE I'M EXITING THE 'ABOVEMENTIONED' MEDITATION

I hear the birds chirping and singing ever louder, the agitated flocks soar over the lake. Eventually I get caught with memories of Ira Cohen, my biggest metaphysical teacher and friend, who lived in India for years. He escaped New York with Paul Bowles, then went to Tangiers. He traveled by boat, a Yugoslav freighter, thus the first Serbian word this renowned American surrealist learned was "nužnik" (toilet) as the boards printed with this word were placed all over the deck.

I remember how Ira described all these incredible and credible flocks of Indian birds in his poems, as he was staying somewhere nearby. Yes, in Pondicherry. He mentioned the bird who sang "*I've got a fever, I've got a fever*" or it sounded like this, phonetically, when it sang. So, this place is a real ashram of souvenirs for me, invading me in huge waves.

There are invasive souvenirs from my youth, but also those from different parts of my life—the Hindus call this sort of quick passing, "smṛti" (Sanskrit: IAST: Smṛti, literally "what's the most important thing to remember while passing out.") But the term also refers to the body of the Hindi text attributed to an author who transcribed a specific traditional legend (and has transferred it to the young).

When I walked into our bungalow I discovered a

certain red box, exactly the same one I owned in my youth, given to me by my mother after I graduated from Belgrade University. I have already thought of that box inadvertently, on the bus mounting towards the Keralayeem. A girl sitting next to me, an Yvvengar yoga instructor, asked me at one point to pay attention to the passing landscape: "You see, all these houses here were built out of red bricks and the bricks curved toward their roof—just like the pagodas," and I thought, yes—just exactly like that red box from my youth! And now, that very box I recalled a few hours prior to coming here, that very box popped out of the darkness of our small cabin.

On the veranda of the neighboring bungalow. I observed a bearded man stretched in a hammock, lying comfortably with his young wife (they must had been Dutch or British). But this young man so reminded me of Beau that I almost screamed out loud—oh, these young, very young people are in fact he and I, transported some 40 years into the future. And this was India and not Africa, however…

The memories started invading me randomly. There was no order to it, no given chronology—while a bright, sunny morning advanced over that huge greenish lake; the tiny boats started circulating up and down the foggy water. One could say—it was bound to become a very hot and beautiful day...

ALLEPPEY

The crazy girls in our bungalow were exchanged for others. The accountant who studies Sanskrit and orders people around left to be replaced by Shirin, a doctoral student in psychology, who also had a great appetite for silk and local jewelry. In front of our bungalow there was a wooden swing installed, somewhat dated and broken, and surely visited by clouds of mosquitoes. Because of these insects, and otherwise, I was more than positive I'd never sit on it or use it in any way. However, Shirin pushed me into an activist's action of repairing the swing so we got into this futility which lasted a good couple of hours. Our super pliable hostesses—the servants of the Keralayeem clad in great purple silken and transparent *saris*—tried to help us by bringing spiral incense which pushed away the mosquitoes; however, the swing could not be repaired.

Our morning was gone; but the whole afternoon we spent at the bazaar of Alleppey, a smaller city not far away from Keralayeem, where the powers of the local rickshaw taxi, popularly called "tuk-tuk" got us. It was a motorcycle connected to a small cabin which was shaking so badly rolling down that local, muddy cobbled road that we managed to taste again our breakfast and lunch nearly vomiting. However, the driving did not last long, perhaps some good twenty minutes. We negotiated the price and cut it down to some hundred drachmas, and as the landscapes swishing by us were so pleasant to look at we soon enough forgot the nausea caused by the rocky road.

In Alleppey itself every private or lively professional activity is being executed on two levels—a street approach to things, treat stands and their banter—and there is another, more private and protected by walls, where everyone speaks the language of air-conditioners. Well, in this one you cannot survive either—it is allegedly more comfortable than the street, but your money purse dies—that is, you get entirely robbed by the 'inside' vendors. In the Alleppey bazaar, I even found those glass bracelets offered to me by madame Sharma so many years ago when she, as the wife of the Indian ambassador to Kaduna, Nigeria, out of her special friendship with my mother-in-law, came personally to greet me the day I, the young Beau's newly-wed wife, arrived in town. She placed them on my hand one after another, these shiny bracelets made of purple and green glass decked in gold (there were perhaps hundreds), and when she reached the lower part of my arm (somewhere just above my elbow) she suddenly looked at me and stopped decorating me (as if some obvious cultural difference became visible and clear to her at that moment).

"So they say in India, my country—be happy and may your marriage be long and fulfilling and may you guys have a lot of children!" she said, smiling one of those large benevolent smiles, speckled with the irregular shining of her gold-filled teeth. To an eighteen-year-old unworldly and inexperienced girl coming directly from Belgrade this custom seemed wild and funny, a bit incredible, filled with the warmth of her smile, which in turn was a reflection of this funny landscape I was to observe in reality only forty years later. This landscape, and the region that fits it, had been already described by Arundati Roy in her novel "The God of Small Things" and was venerated by the French theorist Catherine Clement, herself an ambassador to India, who never failed to call India her true homeland!

The market in Kerala, the first communist state of India, is a far more versatile and abundant version of the Oriental market than that of Marinkova Bara near Belgrade, or the Gypsy-suburb near Parisian Bobigny. However, they do have something in common: they are all decorated with gaudy panels advertising everything. They sell all sorts of goods, that is—everything you can describe in words, and even the products you cannot verbally describe but only convey through smells or colors. There they sell everything, from the tooth-paste which enhances your brilliant golden teeth, to the corn of the Unicorn which enhances man's orgasm—with the Absolute! Here I find also tambourines for one dinar-the instrument is real and well made, and it rightly belongs to this huge circus where everything moves, dances and sings along. Here they sell spice no one has heard of yet, as well as those I have encountered and smelled in my dreams. From then on I have always been able to tell these from other spices; true, I don't know their original names but as "such-and such," I have already smelled this scent and that perfume in one thousand and one Western Oriental stores. Now I can taste it again, buy it for my household and... I have already bought saffron and smelled fresh coriander and cinnamon but here they were not so much market products. They were grown out of this soil, somewhat organically—grown by that muddy road, snatched away quickly then dried and placed for/in the market. Here, kids who sat on their torn-up mats sold them while their fathers, uncles and grand uncles talked and talked, killing lice in their children's hair and selling goods at the same time. You see, these people are not in need, in regards to their own hygiene—they do not worry about sprays and anti-lice lotions nor worry about any other insects which the Jains even respect... You see, there, in the realm where the Europeans stop wanting—they start breathing and enjoying their beloved ART, their so treasured Aesthetics. The Hindus, though they bathe in the river, have no needs—the majority of them are really poor. They eat once a day, sometimes they eat early in the morning, then the following day late at night. Also, they sleep when they can and where they can, on some accessory mat that they find at hand. Poverty and dirt will never make them either sad or upset.

In an Indian hotel where Allen Ginsberg shared a room with Peter Orlovsky in the winter of 1963, the space was so tiny, according to Allen, one could place only a pair of shoes. If they chose to live with a pet, be it a dog or a cat or.... they would have died of asphyxia. There was not enough oxygen. Or as Michaux remarked—the absence of living comfortably does not disturb anyone. People here even despise comfort—what they really need is a lot of air, perhaps "a lot" does not imply some great quantity—let's say just enough air, which they are going to push into their abdomen.

Shiva's temple in Alleppey was unfortunately closed to the public, but as its entrance was so lavishly decorated with numerous lingams, we were able to deduce its interior was a gorgeous enterprise of human cum divine spirit. It was closed, but the thick smell of incense, a mix of sandalwood and patchouli, penetrated the outside and enveloped the temple. I was somehow prepared to see the most stubborn believers leave the temple even at this late hour. I remembered someone said that the only things which really mattered for Hindus are religion and belonging to castes and, that all the rest were just ornaments! I have seen with my own eyes many people at the market, these men with white horizontal lines made of chalk, and wondered, what kind of religious cult they belonged to, what special magic these lines possessed.

Then I remembered, looking and searching for potential believers around Indian temples, Ginsberg and Orlovsky described them as extremely noisy places; they said all of their followers used to sing loudly, and what really caught their attention in particular was the behavior of a certain Brahmin who was loudly singing his hymns and at the same time caressing a cow—so his song, that is, sacred prayers, would also penetrate the animal who couldn't get enlightenment by itself—poor animal that it was, after all. They told me about their sacred odes which they performed to different deities, the songs of the sacred that the chorus of believers sang in Sanskrit. They also couldn't forget those numerous *chandalas* from the caste of the untouchables who would hide themselves in front of the others, even at the moment of dying, as they did not want to be visible and noticed. They would hide their own deaths, they'd usually be encountered behind a temple. The notion of suffering seems not to be relevant to the Hindu. In Europe, if a person is blind or has another handicap he will attract attention from passers-by. Here, in the South of India, one sees mutilated beggars with burnt knees or hands sitting in dusty streets, waiting for passers-by to throw a penny into their bowl. However, it is not certain that they are even waiting for this to happen. There is something so predestined in their destiny that they drag themselves through dust and dirt, semi-paralyzed by their future, sitting on the burnt stubs that used to be their leprous legs or on their crutches they tie to their waist with a piece of string. And of course—their destiny interests neither their rajas, nor the ever more numerous new businessmen of today who are taught by the neoliberal money rat-race how to enter the arena with their American and European competitors. It appears they themselves are even less bothered with their own destinies as they were brought up to follow the ancient Hindu-Buddhist idea that says "the form does not differ from Emptiness and Emptiness is a form in itself." This idea, according to Ginsberg and his pals Burroughs, Kerouac and Snyder, is "the supreme exquisite wisdom" which we find in the texts entitled *Prajnaparamita.* However, for us to understand these texts we have to go through a certain process—a "clearance" of spirit, through its own awakening, the procedure of which enhances our perceptions and improves our vision. Throughout this process we are able to perceive a young sprout as a form of sprout without applying our ordinary, preconceived idea of the future tree, which doesn't allow us to throw a fresh glance at the sprout. It's like, prior to this new experience, we would not allow a new, fresh look full of surprise to be thrust upon that sprout. Some people would name this experience a sudden Gestalt technique, some would call it a particular form of Zen enlightenment known as *satori* which, however, gets interpreted in the West as a specific aesthetic experience.

Ginsberg called this particular experience in poetry

"the direct (subjective or objective) approach to an object." But this approach was announced by Ezra Pound as early as 1912, after an overall influx of Chinese, Confucian and Japanese, as well as Taoist texts made their way into Western literature and philosophy.

Pound's great teacher, Fenollosa, as well as Pound himself, favored the Chinese language, claiming the pictographic alphabet facilitates the "direct way" to the object. The object had already been depicted in the pictograph, thus it was present as a form of hieroglyph in their letters. Pound advocated, as did Ginsberg much later, this Chinese approach to poetry which avoids our so-called Western version of concept, as well as the sentimentality of abstraction in poetry. Both of them pointed to Buddhist poetry where the direct observance of things, without a particular conceptualization, would enter. There was also the clarity and rapidity of seeing an object, as favored by Zen masters, masters of the Tea ceremony, Masters of the Art of Archery and the masters of Gardening.

However, the temple in Alleppey was still mercilessly closed and not a single song could be heard within its walls. Shirin-Rachel and I hail a local rickshaw, and all of a sudden we hear a song: our driver starts singing aloud. It was the hour of his evening prayer and so he's all in his la-la-la mood as he takes us back down that dangerous bumpy road to Keralayeem, without ever thinking for a second that the journey is so drearily unpleasant to us and that we are getting evermore sick and nauseous from the bumps and holes in the road, and oh, that we are so far from enjoying his joyful singing! Now everybody knows that the entire Indian sub-continent sings all the time—from Sri Lanka to the Himalayas, all its peoples drenched in singing. They are rather submerged in some intense and deep feeling and their songs are often sad or simply melancholic. However, I wonder if you can be that sad if you're singing all the time? The European songs which are sad have a nuance of desperation, hopelessness which these songs don't have. The tuk-tuk driver who was at the height of his singing all of a sudden stopped—at the moment he applied the brakes of his motorcycle his song stopped as well, so it felt as if the song was a bit mechanic, as if it worked only with the motorcycle's gas.

The rest of the evening passed sharing dinner with the rest of the group in a dining room of the Keralayeem center. It was in quite a modest, "low profile" fashion, as the French would describe some quiet and unobtrusive event in their own manner. My conversation with Rachel was deep and beautiful (for me personally "depth" always translates to "beauty") as I made the amazing discovery that she was a child of a Persian-Armenian pilot, who was also a Zoroastrian, and a mother of Russian-Jewish background. I recounted the part of my life which prompted me to study Persian Zoroastrianism, so we quickly decided to find a Zoroastrian village here, in this part of India, an event which would mean a lot to both of us but for independent reasons.

We started wondering how it would be feasible—would we be allowed to leave Keralayeem for a while? Would our absence go unnoticed? Would it be visible? Invisible? Inaudible? And above all, acceptable to the rest of that crowd? Our escapade seemed at the same time dangerous and exciting, and above all useful to both of us—our respective life stories inviting us to this kind of miniature trip.

Indian Zoroastrianism has a special history here. After the Islamic conquest of the old Persian empire, the Zoroastrian religion almost disappeared in Persia, but it continued to live in India through a tiny branch of Persians who exiled themselves here. When the Arabs conquered the Sassanian Iran, even in the beginning of the First Caliphate (633 A.D), they started not only exterminating the Zoroastrian population, but pursued burning their books, temples and all the assets of the Sassanian empire. As the Zoroastrians were systematically exterminated in some other countries, it is interesting to note the largest part of this population (some 100 000 inhabitants) is now found in India. They legalized their status by respecting local laws, which prevented them from performing any missionary activity, as well as preventing them marrying outside their community. During a couple of centuries after the Arab conquest,

Zoroastrian merchants were exterminated without mercy: in the 9th century A.D, in China, in the province of Guangzhou, during just one single massacre some 200,000 Persians were slaughtered. The followers of this religion continued immigrating into India but after 1477 this part of the Iranian population, called the Fars, were completely cut off from their original homeland. Three hundred years later they would reestablish contact with their people when in Iran. Under the cruel Qajar dynasty, the non-Muslim population was prosecuted one more time, and the second wave of immigration (the so-called Iranis) started populating Indian lands once again. The Zoroastrians have played quite a significant role in the Indian economic system, as well as the Indian army, especially at the time of the Indian emancipation movement against British colonial rule. For centuries these indomitable warriors and soldiers were well known for their courage. Even today they are known for relentless efforts to retain their land—in Iraq and in Syria, where the Yazidis are almost the only ones to fight fearlessly against the oppression of ISIS.

But how are we going to trace members of such a tribe in Kerala? One thing was sure: the other members of our group were not going to miss us very much—they were all very intimate with one another, after all they had made many trips together prior to this one. They would not include the two of us in any of their conversations, as if we were untouchables. I mean, they appeared untouchable to us because every time Shirin-Rachel and I joined their table they would build a wall of silence between us and them. Or they would discuss fond memories of previous journeys, where she and I were not present, so we would conclude we did not belong to their little club. Even so, I continually insisted my communicative efforts, trying to bridge the gap, this wall of silence, being as I was a big communicator for the Aquarian Mickey Mouse club…

MY FIRST KARMIC DREAM

Certain Tibetan priests claim one has to visit this part of the world in order to experience Karmic dreams. These dreams, they say, give us insight into past lives, as much as they clarify our present and, perhaps, also indicate our favorite period, that is, the future. However, I did not set out on this voyage so that I could follow the instructions of the great Lamas (so-called beginner's *nondro*), although I have met quite a few of these great teachers and received numerous spiritual transmissions from them. As usual, my exploration of a certain geographical region had to be more an anthropological investigation and less a spiritual exercise. However—this is exactly what happened: after my left leg broke in an accident, I started paying attention to my body in quite a Buddhist manner—the experience taught me to be absolutely patient to my bodily needs. I was forced to work out on a daily basis, and my sporting activity contained daily yoga sessions which surely prompted me to go on this particular trip.

Then, all of a sudden it came to me! My first Karmic dream caught me unprepared, that very evening, after Rachel and I discussed our tentative plans for the 'Zoroastrian trip.' We ate a lot of food while chatting and soon went to our bungalow to go to sleep fairly early. But while falling asleep I was still thinking about various possibilities of how to find the Zoroastrians.

So it happened that as soon as I closed my eyes in that bungalow, I had quite a strange dream which served as a partial answer to the unbearably obsessive questions my poor brain had been incessantly asking all day.

In Ferdowsi's well-known epic *Shahnameh Diwan,* dating from the eleventh century, the poet-cum-legendary fighter for a New Persian language, their Vuk Karadžić, gave us a description of the bird *simur,* the fiery bird painted on miniatures and imagined in Oriental and Russian fables. It is enormous, the size of a calf, but in its huge beak carries nothing but its lightest feather! In my dream I see this huge bird carry a white bundle which it drops next to my pillow. Then it turns and takes flight towards Mount Ararat. When I look at the parcel, I see a tiny newborn baby in it!

Soon after, my dear prince charming arrives on this vague plain covered with fog—the one who disappeared from my life because, allegedly, I could not bear a child, a legitimate heir to his royal lineage. Our arguments and disputes lasted years, until one day I decided to run off with a simple gardener, like in Scheherazade's story about prince Shahriar. However, this time I see Farid has entered my dream and rather quickly observed the baby who had landed here; he snatches it away from me placing it in his arms and he immediately starts rocking it to and fro.

"Oh, how happy we should be!" he exclaimed, "here we have the latest descendant of the sultana Mahd-Olia, and our great Qajar dynasty!" "Oh yes," I yawned rather indifferently, "and how I have suffered for years and years to deliver this angel. Remember all the gynecological tests and deadly interventions that cost me health and well-being? The cleansing of the ovaries and constant taking of my temperature during doctor Flamenbaum's, and later doctor Heuzer's, visits. I went through all of this until I reached the office of that wise doctor Gomez who finally decided to leave me and let the powers of nature alone take care of the whole procedure!"

"Aha—but you conveniently forget the torments I had to go through—that torture-chamber where I was tested for sterility, then yes the taking of my temperature as well, before each and every act of love-making so it became some sort of timid, mechanical action… and all those pills I had to swallow in the morning and then again at night," Farid added gloomily, "and all of those mutual efforts and ordeals which did not improve our situation... and look! After all, the seventh miracle has happened, producing this lovely being in a bundle—oh… wait, this is... quite a lovely girl! She is going to be the real Sultana one day. I hope she won't be tempestuous like her mother, Valide Sultana, sitting next to us! Yes, she is going to be her father's little girl, his pride, the goddess Athena incarnated, born from Zeus's head, the real grand-grand-daughter of Abbas Shah, the loveliest Taj Olsulta. Hey, the one who conquered and modernized Iran—she did that right after she conquered her own father… and you know how she managed to do that?" (Farid was quite elaborate on this particular occasion, like on any other, but even more than before. He was a real philosopher of the post-Kantian orientation who liked to give his words an extra weight) "She did it by quoting the words of Cyrus the Great, 'If I conquer the world, it will be for its own good—that world will solely benefit from such victory!'" "And then he threw the baby in the air. Luckily it landed back in his arms, "Oh, my Sultana! Please tell me how this unique and lovely being came to us! How did it happen, after all this time?"

"Well, perhaps you won't like my story," I hesitated, "but the baby was dropped off here by a *simur*, the legendary flyer, who flew in through this window and simply placed the baby on my lap." I felt utterly exhausted.

He smiled at me, using one of his thirteen incredibly charming smiles, and that was enough for me to stop being angry. That very second I simply stopped being angry, for everything, for of all those things I had already summed-up one million times prior to this event.

One—the fact he'd left for San Francisco leaving me alone to shriek with ravens and vultures in Paris, the coldest city in the world. He was nothing more than a Persian prince from the Qajar dynasty, so he treasured his descendants more than anyone or anything else in the world.

Two, three, four, etc.—And it is not true he got mad at

me, at a certain moment, for escaping from his garden with Masoud, his gardener. In fact he felt utterly defeated and forlorn because I was not physically fit to give him an heir.

In the book, "One Thousand and One Nights," prince Shahriar goes to hunt and his sultana, once she turned three times around in order to be safe and sure there were no other beings but the roses and gazelles in her garden, called the name of her unfortunate black gardener: "Masoud, oh, Masoud! Come sprinkle my private garden, oh my beloved one!"

Just to mention here my story was not much different from that ancient one. The prince had forgotten something at the palace, so he returned quickly from the hunt and once he reentered the garden he was bound to see lovers entwined.

No, he never forgave me my debauchery, my thirst for the black, naked body of that idiot servant, Masoud, until that moment in my dream. He seemed to have forgiven me my idiocy. He also stopped being angry with me, for everything, for all those things I already summed up nicely one million times prior to this event.

"Oh, you will see," his words rushed out suddenly, "my mother Mimi, the grand-daughter of the most illustrious sultana Mahd-Olia, is going to open her treasury—we won't starve ever again. Mother is certainly going to allocate huge monthly sums for the occasion..."

Our disputes over money and daily existence had

become dreadful. I met Farid just after his father died in Iran, which he dared to reenter after long exile, in 1998. As the former personal doctor of the Shah Reza Pahlavi, he was never well received in Revolutionary Iran, nor by the Pahlavi, as he was married to a Qajar. Moreover, Farid's mother always claimed the Pahlavi's themselves killed his father in Tehran. As soon as the funeral was over, Farid's mother, Mimi, froze their inheritance money in American and Swiss bank accounts "so that the boys would not spend the money lavishly." As a result, during the time we first met, Farid's life was very modest and almost too meagre in Paris. As I did not know who he was and where he came from, I invited him right away to move into my place and shared whatever I had at that moment. His way of thinking was so exceptional, so compatible with my own that I believed it was the sky itself which made our encounter possible. And the words he spoke, just like one of Scheherazade's stories, were falling out of his mouth, turning immediately into pearls, so I started building up necklaces for myself out of these words, and look here—at all these jewels I'd placed around my neck right there in my dream, as we were speaking and rocking the baby at the same time.

I stopped breathing as heavily under this jewelry as I used to, and I stopped trying to take it off my neck, as I used to. I just began yelling again, relentlessly, like I did that day the electricity and phone company cut off their services at the same time. That very day, in a semi-lit apartment, I tried to question him about the succession of the dynasties of the Persian empire.

"Was the Persian court cruel?" I ask and he answers with a smile, that well-kept superior smile of his.

"Of course it was cruel. It was, it has been, it is—today, just like it was in the past. See what they've done to Soraya!?

"How so, what have they done?" I'm asking him, surprised. "Didn't she kill herself with drugs and alcohol?"

He starts eyeing me attentively. "Oh no, she was such a well-bred German girl of Iranian ancestry. But as she was the Shah's first wife, so-called Valide Sultana, she was meant to give him heirs and she failed to do so. I do think the Shah killed her, but indirectly—he divorced her, and as she loved him it was like a death sentence to her. He sent her to an eternal, European exile."

"Aha, it sounds like Ivo Andric's story, 'Devil's Yard'!" I took the book off the shelf and opened it to a page which talks about Jem Sulan and his exile, as retold a century later by a certain Chamil who was tortured by the Sultan's secret police in that very yard.

"Oh, give me the book, Sultana! Do you guys write "çem" with a "j", so it's like—Jem (Sultan)?" he asked.

"Ah yes, the Turks were nomads and simpletons who took all their refinements from the Persian court—those asses did not even know what a plot and a counter-plot meant in diplomacy. They were very poor spies. They say they used a "silk belt" to suffocate the enemy, but they did not even know what a belt was, and silk was also an unknown fabric. However, Andric knows things kept repeating through the ages. These plots against kings and their citizens were also popular at the time of OZNA. And there was Selimovic, yes, I like that one, in that book "Dervish and His Death" where the old Dervish… well, we have that motif in our great Sadegh Hedayat, the story about the death of our last Zoroastrian king..."

"So you think Soraya was killed by Savak or an organisation like that," I asked quietly, sad at this discovery.

"Yes, and she was replaced by Farah Diba who gave the Shah the Royal princes."

Now I kept silent. Somehow it was dawning at me that both Andric and Selimovic spoke of modern times through the respective mouths of the dervish and Chamil. Was it the era of the "Inform-bureau" in Yugoslavia? Of course it was always the same method of removing an ill-suited candidate.

"We won't talk about death, Sultana," suddenly he decided, "let us go and take a walk through the Luxembourg gardens..."

"No, I won't hear a word about the walk in the gardens, you're just changing the issue! And don't think that we will ever get anything from Mimi, my dear, she is a great Turskish *banu,* (aristocratic lady) so she won't bother to give this child anything, she will not do it!"

Me and my silly insistence on anything. I was stubborn as any other janitor. But I was wrong to set fire against my mother-in-law who liked me somehow, this I was sure of although I could never be 100 percent sure of anything.

"She is going to send us a box of cookies from Shiraz, that fabulous city where Jalal-al-Din hid his suite before the decisive battle with the Tatars and Moguls in that distant 1226." I rolled my French consonants quickly, as always when angry, "this is what she's going to do. Just wait. She's going to send a box of chocolates, or send a carpet to her grand-daughter—she will do it, and perhaps, honestly, that would be a decent gift from her—from someone who's in such a fragile and uncertain situation."

I was yelling so loud, feeling the surplus of emotions invading me like a mad wave, that after a few seconds, from all that inner noise and agitation I woke.

Darkness and quiet reigned in the bungalow, interspersed here and there with the chirping of the unusual crickets. I've just had this strange Karmic dream that convinced me the Sultan was still in the back of my mind, that he never left his place. It reminded me of my own stupid mistakes, they were big existential wrong moves I made in life and oh, Lo, I knew they were uncorrectable. So this whole process was dumb and unnecessary—why would anyone torture himself/herself with faulty errors and mistakes s/he made if they were not to be corrected but were instead coming back only to further upset me? The moral of my ten-year-long story with Sultan could be summed up like this: whenever I cannot correct my own mistakes I should let go of the feeling of self-hatred because one cannot correct a thing which has always been incorrigible. I should always be gentle with the person who hurt me and eventually forget the fact we had fought a battle, because eventually there always comes a *simur*, at one point or another, carrying a solution in its beak. That solution we should take as the right one and be ready to accept it just at the split second when the *simur* is about to land and we intercept the bundle…

I had been quite awake for a while when I found myself crawling across the bungalow looking for a battery torch in the dark. It was exactly 3:30 am. It was perhaps the midnight hour in Europe and I observed my sheets were thoroughly wet with sweat. The air was impregnated with humidity and through that humid air, one could overhear the ominous buzz of the armies of hungry mosquitoes. It seemed they were perfectly able to penetrate the security net of the palanquin above our beds, and my assumption was perfectly correct. The palanquin was full of holes which allowed millions of insects to get through, so in a way there was no reason for us to keep that tattered net above our heads. And the air, which was sparse under this net was so humid and unbearable that the net itself did not improve our condition. On the contrary, it just worsened it.

THE VERY NEXT DAY

Early that morning I heard a light pounding on my door. It was not Rachel—she had left earlier that morning—and in front of me there were these three beautiful girls clad in light purple raw silk and they were smiling, always smiling, eyeing me cautiously and talking among themselves in Malayan. One of them, the oldest in that group, became very happy at learning I spoke English. The centuries of British civilization had left a trace in this country, the equivalent of a huge purple stain which neither Gandhi nor Nehru could clean out or erase.

"Madam, how long are you going to stay in your bungalow this morning? We were ordered to begin cleaning the cabins, starting with your room first."

While she was tweeting softly with her Malayan accent, she was turning her head left and right, which was so different from our nodding, and meant something entirely different from our Western 'approval' and 'disapproval', as their writers communicated to me much later.

"Well, of course, the room is completely yours, and I am running completely late for my morning yoga class—everyone has taken their mats to the center. I am the only one who sleeps this late, however, look girls our place is so untidy. I'm afraid you won't be able to manage it yourselves. Can I help you with anything, girls?"

All three of them laughed out loud—probably no one, in their long experience as cleaning ladies happened to ask them such a question! My question was really merely polite, but it seemed these girls were shocked to see anything gentle, any polite expression coming from a European, or let's just say from a white person.

Michaux said once that whites possess a certain quality of soul which pushed them very far on the long road to their civilization, but this particular quality was nothing but boldness or impertinence, which implied basic disrespect toward the Other. Being very different from them, the Hindus are quite religious which means they deeply respect others and human beings as such. There are also the Americans who are a mixture of them all. They are likely to possess all the human qualities of all races in a huge spectrum as, generally speaking (and how I hate to generalize!) they lack something in their real spirituality. They exaggerate everything, especially their aptitude to embrace almost all forms of religious syncretism. Well, it is really Michaux who is the origin of such a claim, but I had witnessed the fact in that I personally met many decent, spiritual, intelligent but socially underprivileged North Americans, who could teach the rest of the crowd, especially Europeans, how to be impartial, human, and very profound while relating to others. And here, there are Indians, the representatives of the old Vedic tradition, their pariahs included, who appear noble, dotted with a certain elegance of spirit as they are mostly silent and unobtrusive—perhaps qualities they have gained through physical suffering and the pain of the underdog.

Almost all of us agree the most moving moment in the history of Buddhism is not the appearance of Buddha's mysterious smile, but the appearance of his tear. Thus I think Michaux was right when making a colonialist remark both the Arabs and the Indians, even those of the chandalas' order, were "impregnated with dignity as they carry their clothes, carry themselves, their turbans—they carry them upright, with dignity and they are proud of it." The Europeans appear sad, second-hand and beat when compared to them. Perhaps the French author declared all this because he never had a chance to meet our Montenegrin who are also tall and distant and elegant, but in a way differing from the Orientals.

However, it seems in their elegance and natural posture there is an important element of practicality—the Indians and the Arabs are not really concerned for their good looks, as they consider the aesthetics of appearance a transitory movement, just a step up the ladder leading them to the Absolute; the sense of beauty does not represent to them some essential quality in a man—they keep upright and do yoga because that keeps them healthy and in a beneficial physical condition. Their body is light and supple as it carries a spine which does not curve and bows—they do not know the painful effects of scoliosis; their muscles are strong as they make prostrations while praying so their muscles and their skin are almost always firm. Perhaps all religions are practical and utilitarian this way—the Muslims and the Jews do not eat pork, it is forbidden to them because of the hot climate they live in. Pork gets spoilt easily in hot weather so as soon as it was cooked it becomes an awful nutritional bomb filled with bacteria. For the same reason a hot climate, boys get circumcised in those regions. Why didn't the Christians adopt this ancient custom? Perhaps they have mostly lived in colder climates where the humans as well as animals were not exposed to the quick development of bacteria.

My anthropological meditation floated far, far down into the greenish marsh where I found myself seated on a boat overlooking the stale and sluggish water. Then all of a sudden, an unusual animal head rising above the water caught my glance. It was hard to tell if it was the head of an alligator or a crocodile, I was not sure which one it was in this muddy habitat. I've never been an expert in reptiles.

I could relate though to its attitude towards personal hygiene and aesthetics. The Indians, so much like alligators, tend to their habitat, their home, which seems more important to them than their own good looks. I've seen it with the Roms. The members of this forlorn and cheeky nomadic Indian tribe, just as their ancestors the Indian rajas and other sedentary cousins like to keep their own private abodes tidy and decorated. Regardless if they reside in a tent or a palace while on earth, they treat their bodies as the extended households of their beings. When the Indian wishes to decorate his interior he embellishes his mind through meditation. He is intense and practical and therefore wishes to remain healthy; he is the first ascetic. He also renounces so many things he might as well be athletic as he attends to his magic rituals. However, he would be the first one to introduce electricity to his household in order to keep it clean. It is impractical to get sick in this country where all the believers take their baths in the Ganges, the river which accepts them naked, squating, or floating in their prayers, physically addressing the Absolute. For the Roms though, as much as for the Indians, beauty is an affair which belongs to the Baroque. It is lush, enormous and ample: their Pantheon is an exaggerated arabesque, quavery and seductive. Thus their oversized love for detail, sidepieces, codes, figures, religious symbols, even the grammar itself. Michaux visited a museum in Colombo and there he claimed was only one room a Westerner could take in without disgust—the room with local frescoes from Sigeria, and the rest, according to him, was trash. See how everything is relative in this world: when I was in the Louvre I happened to view most of the neoclassical rooms with disgust. I didn't feel better in the rooms with the Impressionists either, where tidy order and hygiene were even more prominent than in these orderly Indian houses. However, it is true that the population here was the first one to divide people into classes and castes. They invented the notion of the raja, the king, but also the notion of the servant. Those members of the blind caste of helpless and obedient slaves persuaded, for centuries, to be at peace with their status quo and not to rebel against it, as they were born only to serve others, and that was it.

This attitude, which is somewhat on the defensive side, has contributed to the fact that they have remained victims throughout many centuries. Alexander the Great subdued them, then different Greek kings, the Huns, the Moguls and finally the Brits, who overstayed in India and left these people their appetite for high capitalism as heritage. Still, there is an enigma that I cannot solve: how did these wise and ancient civilized peoples remain such cowards in front of their enemies as if they feared life? And if you ask a Hindu such a question he will laugh it off and give you a magnificent comparison: when a royal elephant becomes scared of a tiny branch standing in its way he turns around and starts running back and the entire royal army follows. However, the elephant is a quiet animal whose character does not scare so easily. He is whimsical, moody, more sensitive than a horse or a camel and those who are accompanied by him know he can get enraged easily. People know how vengeful he can be and when he remembers something that's usually for life. We remember different stories retold by the animaltamers in circuses who recall an elephant, offended by its trainer, all of a sudden killed him thirty years after the event. However, I stood in this dark bungalow, a bit lost to circumstance. I was trying to think up a way to get rid of these cordial serving ladies. In fact, to be honest, they really started bothering me as they were just at the point of ignoring my freedom-loving attitude and independent thinking; independent from any domestic service. I believed in self-reliance like any damn given anarchist on earth. I hated any form of behavior which resembled "serving" someone or something, but these innocent ladies could not fathom the bottom of my heart.

So they started questioning me "…is there anything wrong with the service, madam?" Did I find their help inadequate? I told them I was happy to see them here, but I would be even happier to see them conduct some other business elsewhere.

Now all three of them stared at me in bewilderment and in order to soothe their trauma I said I'd like to photograph them together, as a souvenir of my visit. In fact, it would be awesome if someone could take a photo of the four of us together. There we go, we would look someone up, someone who could take such a snapshot—and who could that be? No one else but our dear Michelle in person, the lady whom we met right at the beginning of my trip and who could not get into my interest in different schools of Buddhism. She was just passing by, as she decided not to attend a yoga class that morning. Her weight was a real impediment for her, so she wandered around, wondering if there was any other person who stayed out of class like her. Yes, that person was me, and she was eager to know why I'd stayed in the bungalow that morning. "I hope you're safe and sound," she cheerfully exclaimed! "I'm coming over to take you to the beach—I see your interest for yoga has expired!"

"To the contrary! Miii-chelle! I overslept and I feel guilty for it, but perhaps you and I could get our daily yoga asanas done at the beach? But first, Michelle, you have to take a couple of pics of me and these lovely girls here!" She was more than happy to do it, partially because she was scared I would force her, now, to do all these postures that she had escaped this morning, so all this resulted in her taking one million extra photos of us all. And if we were to print all her numerous snapshots we'd be able to fill several photo albums, bigger in size than those containing the pics of tiny new-borns which proud parents senselessly stock in their attics.

The cleaning ladies were quite confused with this unexpected amount of attention lavished on them. I equally remembered Michaux and his reticence at being served by all his servants on his trip through Asia. He was constantly making an effort to explain to them that he wasn't a maharajah, not a nabob, not a European aristocrat either. In doing so he was emphasizing the fact that they should not try hard to please him as he was never going to be reborn an Indian. "The less you try to please me, the happier I am," he would add. He could not stand to see them making prostrations in front of him, nor see the cook serving him as if he were a prince. He was growing desperate when the servants were blindly obeying him in Bombay and he accused the Brahman caste for having taught the massive population the virtue of total obedience for over two thousand years. As soon as he arrived in India he understood there was yet another caste, "the untouchables", who were crossing the street with a bell tied to their necks exclaiming loudly "Move, oh, ye, noble people so the scum can cross this road!"

Not only were these wretched ones forbidden to enter the temples but they could not be employed to do the dirtiest jobs on earth. They kept putting themselves down as often as they were mutilating themselves, exclaiming all along that they would never attain the *real God.*

Michaux hated Brahmins with all his heart and he remarked as they despised and tortured the rest of the population, they probably nourished a hidden hatred for themselves. At the time he visited India there was a certain Renasanri Naiker in Madras who founded an association of *self-respect* that tried to gather lower castes without Brahmins, who were literally forbidden to join in. But even in Michaux's time it was forbidden for the pariahs to ride on the train with other passengers and they also continued to tie a string around their waist, a sign of their low status. The descendants of the Brahmans continued to show arrogance in their behavior. At the time Michaux visited one of their universities, he asked a Hindu eminent professor of Sanskrit and a connoisseur of music, to explain certain aspects of poetry sung in the north of India and Nepal. However, his Indian colleague not only refused to help Michaux but exclaimed something that put the Frenchman ill at ease: "Why would I throw pearls before swine?" To which the high-spirited author responded those who constantly keep the pearls for themselves turn eventually into swine themselves.

The day had advanced and I began rushing with my friend to see the beach which was beautiful and savage, endless dunes and high waves. The tuck-tuck driver was in a deep slumber under the farthest palm tree, waiting for us to join him. The bank lady was screaming in pain all the way down the road to the beach. The road itself was heavy, cobbled and in serpentines. Michelle had already seen herself in hospital, with all her bones fractured and thus she continued with her incessant "auch, auch, auch". One would have thought someone was cutting her to pieces. As soon as we arrived on the beach she rushed to a local stand, got herself a fat sandwich and then she was OK. The ocean had a soothing effect on me and the driver was also soothed by his own meditation under a palm tree, as well as the knowledge that soon enough he would be rewarded with a couple of rupees for his patience and suffering with us.

The Indian Ocean is very warm on this Southwestern side, but it is also unpredictable and wild. I would pass this winter undisturbed by the urban flu because I walked through this ocean in my pants, which lift me up, like a wave and carry through to the next season! The evening meditation in Keralayeem was beautiful, it bore all the nuances of this orange-purple sky which I observed quietly as the evening descended upon the ocean. And all these creatures, otherwise called my traveling companions, became calm and contemplative, but as they say—that's what contemplation is all about.

THE SECOND KARMIC DREAM

That night, in a stuffy bungalow, I had my second karmic dream, which was somewhat easier than the first as it was filled with colors, stretched canvases, and brushed half-clean with the obtrusive smell of turpentine. As if all the colors of the sky were washed out by the ocean that entered my dream, as well as did enter all the nuances of a wild sunset. I was sitting in the bathtub of my Roman friend, Enzo Cucchi, in his big studio of Villa del Orso, while he was sitting behind me getting ready to draw a portrait of me. "Enzo, Enzo!" I exclaimed all excited, as I became confused by the sight of something I saw in front of me, "don't you see these colored pencils which keep growing out of my fingers, oh, brother! What am I going to do, mutilated as I am?"

He looked at me with his deep eyes—he would always look long, significant and deep whenever he had something important to say—and then he whispered slowly: "You should use this unusual event to your own benefit. That means you have to draw more often, don't you confuse the issues, baby, the real "Arte Povera" artist is you and not me! You are not only poor, "povera" but you have an enormous talent as we have been reminded of here, that should be put to use! Look here, yesterday when I ran into our friend Bonito Oliva, I showed him one of your drawings but I didn't tell him who made it, so the old man started praising my talent. It was the drawing in which you're drawing my head while I'm drawing you and this is somehow all about the fact the drawing was overlooking me while I was making it, and moreover Oliva mentioned the fact my 'subject and themes improved as I did not insist on those vague spaces overflowing.' In other words, I wasn't into "Cucchi's landscapes" any longer, but thinking, reflecting on the painting while creating it listening to what the creation was whispering to me instead of forcing my will upon it."

"But wait," I interrupted his dream-stream. "You are absolutely right when you insist on my working on a project, as I know I shouldn't just sit in your bathtub and wait for your flow of inspiration to come our way. I don't want to be your muse any longer—it's a totally boring and inadequate role for me. Even if my talent was small or quite big as you have just indicated five minutes ago—it's not quite cool for me to sit here lounging and doing basically nothing while waiting for providence to shower new opportunities on me."

"Would you like an ice-cream, Muse?" he interrupted, aware I had a hidden weakness for that frozen sugar. The weakness would usually invade me in an early Roman afternoon, about the time I moved to his studio.

"Ice-cream or not, now, please listen to me. Every day I happen to admire your ability to work undisturbed by all other invading circumstances as you always find time to paint… but I cannot follow you. I get too absorbed by all other existential problems which start pounding at my head like a hammer, and I know if I were to draw and paint more seriously than I'm doing now, soon enough I'd be worried about how to sell my work, then I'd worry how to find a gallery-owner or some other small fry to sell it for me—and my creativity would turn into sheer nightmare—yes, that's the way I am."

Enzo laughed on very rare occasions, especially since his ex-wife and their son finally said good-bye. But this time, at least in this dream, I squeezed something out of him which resembled a grin.

"Well, don't you worry about selling your stuff, that procedure has nothing to do with our activity, although I will admit here with you that the so-called great artists are great because, among other things, they know how to advertise and sell their artwork. This activity, unfortunately, has proven to be the greatest art of them all! But what I suggest here is that under each and every drawing you make you sign my name beneath and whoops—you'll see, you will be able to sell them easily."

"Oh, I do not want it this way!" I retorted angrily. "This would not be fair nor correct either to you or to me, not to mention the person who buys it—that would be simply disgusting!"

I jumped out of the bathtub and ran to the kitchen.

"Don't go, hey, come back! I don't want to stay here without my favorite model to whom I'm just about to give a form to a huge green balloon, hey, c'mon, stay with me. What's wrong? Believe me—no one will ever figure out that you were the model for this green thing!"

"Ha! Don't panic, silly, I'm just going to get an ice-cream," I said laughingly, my head half-submerged in the fridge. But our dialogue had hurt me, and why and how it did—this I could not explain. I was sitting in his studio in Via del Orso for a while, my head dipped in his fridge or in his bathtub, that is. I was getting dressed up for certain occasions. I would accompany him on his walks to cafe Rosati and back while my parents, being extremely worried, were sending me tons of letters and telegrams reminding me the last hour had arrived to come back home. What they meant by "home" though, I could not fathom. I did not feel like going back to New York because its noise and filth had started to profoundly get on my nerves. And I had no courage for returning to Belgrade. I had left my hometown so long ago now it looked like an entirely new city to me—a place where even sparrows sing differently from those sparrows of my childhood. At any rate I was not ready to go "back" to any place I should have to one more time and all over again get used to new bathtubs and fridges with their special instructions in numerous languages.

And in fact, Rome wasn't my favorite city of them all: too much of everyone's past, both common and private histories accumulated there. It was catholic, dated, very rigid. It killed Pasolini and even Enzo did not feel at home in it, because if he did I wouldn't be prancing in his bathtub like a frozen fish right now while his small boy, Alessandro, was waiting for him in another part of town. The boy was waiting for him to show and take him for a walk his dad would never take him for. It was as if this bathtub accumulated all the sad childhoods in this world... and there was this air—this tub and in Villa Borghese, in the Colosseum and even further out in the suburb EUR, some Roman version of New Belgrade built by Mussolini. This one was looking for the stable kitch of Neoclasicism everywhere, and built his City in EUR. The air extended even further, to the beaches of Ostia, it was suffocating me everywhere. So then I see myself with my fingers that extend into colored pencils, tearing my stockings while putting them on, and putting on my T-shirt upside down so I could finally reach for my pants and my shoes. I caught the last glimpse of my bag buried somewhere, which I grabbed and was then ready to leave.

"Wait a minute, darling", he merely whispered, "it seems you are in a hurry to leave?"

"Oh, no, not really. I'm just going out to get some ciggies, do you need anything from downstairs?"

"It's January, crazy woman, put your coat on, at least!"

I left that coat in Rome and, semi-naked, jumped into a fast train leaving the Termini station just at the moment I got there. I arrived in Venice five hours before one of my grand-mothers, Olga, died. Most of her time she was staring at something in front of her, gasping at the Grand Void. I had found the hospital in Venice and my grandma in it, with great difficulty, as I only vaguely remembered the address my parents sent to me three months earlier.

Luckily, as soon as I arrived she recognized me and smiled gently at me. "You are not of this world, are you?" she whispered barely audibly into my ear. And then "You are that angel who came to fetch me and take me to that other world," she spoke loudly this time, munching and slurping her words down as old people sometimes do.

"Oh, no, I would not say I am that person, grandma, but tell me, how do you recognize angels?" I asked her, tears rolling down my cheeks. I should have left Enzo's tub much, much earlier that winter and stayed here, beside her.

"Look here," she made a considerable effort to lift her head from her pillow, an endeavor which bordered on the impossible, but she was obviously trying to give her words some additional weight.

"When you see above someone's head a thin golden ray of light..." she stopped in the middle of the sentence and her head fell back to the pillow from the heavy effort. Those were the last words she uttered. I stayed with her for the next couple of hours in the hospital filling out death certificates and then I left.

I woke and found myself in the Indian bungalow in Keralayeem, which was still dark. However, there was a thin golden ray dimly perched on one of its walls; this ray was arching the door leading to the bathroom. All of a sudden I felt very light, weightless—something very strange, like a very light fever was shaking my whole body but I had already decided not to pay attention to it. I was actually trying to fall into sleep again but the sleep wouldn't come back.

On the night table, just next to me, there is a moody torchlight which, due to bad contact probably, constantly goes off and on, so there is no way I can get any reading done. I am trying to breathe in and out, to forget Italy altogether while the mosquitoes keep buzzing ominously through the room lit by the golden dust.

EVERY MORNING

We were doing Hatha yoga which some people in Germany or France could easily call by now "their daily TV commercial gymnastics," but here it was something else. I imagine everyone goes to India in order to recall what these real classes in yoga look like, in their natural habitat of course. There were many. Controlled breathing is part of the Indian national tradition.

Michaux enthusiastically recalls an event that occurred while he was waiting for a train at the Serampora station. He ran into a *baba* there and asked him how to breathe in and breathe out the air, that is, how to meditate. Three minutes later they were surrounded by bank tellers, counselors, students and all sorts of people breathing air in and out, and at the same time trying to explain to our writer the main principles of an *ujjayi*. Watching the master of meditation pumping his stomach with air was an experience of the greatest importance to Michaux, the best one he had in India so far. The master would collect the air "from the above" extremely slowly as if he were drying out a wet object. Then he would push that air into his lungs, then into his stomach, all the way to his genitals. When the stomach of the master began to resemble a ball or the head of a fetus, it would soon be ready to flatten completely. The inhalation lasts a long time with this teacher, Michaux explains, as he was careful not to hurt his inner organs, which can happen with this exercise. *Ujjayi* can hurt people easily, like a knife if we do not know how to direct it "towards our inner being"—which in this master remained very young as he looked like a teenager in his old age, probably due to all the air he inhaled, the author jovially remarks. Michaux describes this master as a being lifted beyond any form of human suffering, uplifted and flying beyond any casual event around him—indeed, not because he would be indifferent to it but because he was inhabited by some real "goodness." He was marked by an expression of soft sadness, like those handicapped people who have suffered a certain deformity from their birth.

Our teacher here is not like the one Michaux described in his book. Perhaps he is an Indian in his soul and perhaps he was even one of them in his previous lifetimes, but in the present one he looks like a real Frenchman. We are following Renan's asanas though, according to his precise instructions. He entitled our expedition "Krisna's training."

Since the times when I was attending several retreats with the great Tibetan lamas (I met something like thirty of them in a period of over twenty years), I haven't felt so much joy, so much pleasure—but also a certain boredom in the given activities. Half of my fellow-travelers here are trying, panicked, to lose some weight. They stubbornly try, in a mad effort to perform exhausting *ashtangas* done in succession, jumping to and fro, and then once they become thoroughly exhausted and in pain, they seek someone to perform Ayurveda massage on them! They are massaged around noon and in the afternoon they continue purifying their breath; they breathe in and exhale that humid air, all that petite-bourgeois world from the 16th Parisian arrondissement, so that they can go in the evening to *darshan*, a visit or homage to the Great Ama, a woman Guru who has already embraced 8,000,000 people. Or they go and buy and buy and buy all sorts of souvenirs. I join this last group, although it's more than predictable one of these local vendors is going to hack my bank account.

While we are buying one and a thousand and one spices in the shop of perfumed oils and spices, I try to pay for merchandise with my credit card which is apparently blocked. I hire a rickshaw to take me to the nearest bank machine and that happens to be a real hole in the wall cemented by mud in the worst dilapidated log cabin in the small town of Alepi. Alas, I cannot take money from that machine either, and then I get the information concerning my whole murky case, directly and *ex machina*, as they say. My Credit Lyonnais bank calls me from Paris asking me to block my account so they wouldn't be forced to do it. They had observed some suspicious activities, as if I were simultaneously taking the money from the account and at the same time crediting it, multiplying my deposits only to take a credit out of this bank. All in all, they knew I was in India but not really acting myself, *as if I were not I but someone else*, and these transactions did not resemble my usual banking habits. The best thing was to freeze my account until I returned to Paris, so that we could continue our "collaboration." I started counting my coins. As I've heard a number of stories about the abuse of credit cards and bank accounts of those who traveled to India I was cautious enough to save a small sum of some 50 euros and put it in my caftan coat before the very beginning of our trip. In fact, I hid this cash even from myself as I put it in the most distant and hidden pocket of my coat. Now I was more than glad I had done so. So much the better—I'll stop buying souvenirs, silk scarves, silver leg bracelets, bronze Ganesha statues and other trinkets. The cupboards of all my cousins and all my friends are already filled with these silly objects anyways... The only thing someone had brought from India worth mentioning was an instrument—Allen's ancient Indian harmonium. A prototype of our contemporary accordion that was a heavenly instrument, capable of making a pig forget his porcine character by lifting it up to heaven.

Today is December 31 and under the hot Kerala sun we are supposed to celebrate the New Year. We did our morning yoga practice accompanied by perfect *pranayama*, strict breathing exercises, and then some dozen of us boarded a small boat that swallows liters of gasoline circling the canals and local islands. It's trips of this sort I like the best. Usually the trips are short, they are not tiring, so I remember them as I've had a similar experience floating down the Nile all the way from Cairo to Aswan. I wonder why I like to repeat experiences and why I always try to find similarities between these events on all different trips. However, floating down or up this marsh is a unique experience. As the Hindus do everything slowly their boat also moves slowly and stops by the bank all the time.

The Yogis are very economical in using their proper energy and Michaux was right to call them "übermensch" as they never reach the point of exhaustion, never reach that deeply painful spot in themselves which is the source of a certain dynamism in us. They simply avoid it. They are, in fact, enraptured by ancient and epic drowsiness, say, slumber. And so is our boat captain to whom this whole one-day trip along the ten-mile-long canal means nothing but the accomplishment of his own peaceful momentum, as he did it for his own pleasure. It was his own ode to tranquility.

I remembered then our Egyptian captain who was taking us on a boat named "Cleopatra" from Luxor, via Abu Simbel, to the dam of Aswan. He was able to navigate a good couple of hundred miles up and down the Nile just in one single afternoon! True, on our trip to Aswan we were not encountering the coconut palms which were so numerous here in Kerala, that the habit of our Indian captain to stop the boat, cut a coconut off a tree and drink its milk, was quite understandable. This adventure was about to last the whole afternoon, so, good luck with it. Let our New Year's Eve be quiet and beautiful, like the rest of the afternoon.

Tired from heavy *ashtanga* exercises that were meant to please the Gods that morning, my fellow-travelers were now pouncing greedily on coconuts. As they drank enormous quantities of that fruity milk, people like the fragile Myriam, fat Michelle, or the student of Sanskrit, started complaining of stomach aches. It prolonged our trip ad infinitum as these ladies would never lie down in the grassy field, notwithstanding performing their toilet needs out there. So they looked for toilets everywhere, prolonging our journey, like I said, beyond proportion! They would hide themselves somewhere on one of these islands, then return to the boat, and then, oh yes, listen to me carefully now: they would ask the captain to stop the boat again so he could cut new coconuts for them one more time. In this way they continued the vicious circle: they would drink the coconut milk, then would howl with stomach pains, then stop the boat in order to find a toilet, then they would get back on the boat and promptly ask the captain to anchor the boat and cut some new nuts for them, and cut them nicely so they could drink that stuff one more time.

When my Western-cum-Byzantine patience had finally expired here, I addressed a good-natured owner of a luxury shop in Montmartre called Pierre, who was often standing next to me, eyeing me benevolently all this time. His huge belly was shaking up and down, following the movement of the boat's noisy engine.

"This is becoming unbearable! How do you take all this, Pierre?"

He smiled back at me while commenting loudly: "Ah, you haven't done your meditation correctly today, Nina. I see that many things are bothering you..."

Then he added in the same peaceful fashion: "We cannot blame our ladies for desiring all that coconut milk, as this is the only thing we will be having tonight for our New Year's evening!" Overhearing our conversation our neighbor, the ever-curious Sally, the student of Sanskrit, exclaimed in disbelief: "Wait a minute, Pierre, I know from my confidential sources somewhere in the village we can find alcohol. Can you go for instance a bit further down to the village bush and look for the guys selling it? If you could get us at least a bottle … here, I'm going to collect money right away!" Pierre seemed happy as a lark. For the French, any festivity, especially the celebration of New Year's, without alcohol seems like a major trial and tribulation in Hell to which no single, personal meditation could serve as remedy. They were not prepared for this final blast here, so they were all secretly nervous and disappointed that they couldn't get a glass of any alcohol tonight, a situation that could never occur at this time in the wine-loving country France.

I was rather skeptical, "I have to remind you, my friends, that a bottle of whiskey on the black market in

Libya could reach the price of 150 dollars, well, a while ago."

"Oh, come on, Nina, it's not your day today, you're seeing all things in the negative! I will go to that village right away. This situation is really unbearable to all of us."

As soon as he announced his readiness, the unreasonable commands started flowing in from all directions: "I would like a bottle of Fitou," and then, "I would rather go for some Bordeaux." Michelle desired only Burgundy, and Renan was just watching all the commotion created around him when, at the given moment he spoke, advising Pierre to take very little money with him because "some tourists were looking for alcohol here a while ago only to be ripped off, abused verbally and physically by the local population," etc.

Needless to say, Pierre's search for the Holy alcohol ended exactly as Renan had predicted. Michaux himself had also nicely reminded the reader in his book that people who travel to India for the first time have to leave aside some of their old, preconceived notions: one of these was the idea that they would meet on their journey some Indian intellectuals, and the other—that they would find any alcohol. For the first fantasy, Michaux says, it was good for us to remember that their learned men hide in the cities and come out to the countryside or travel their roads only when they go on their 'retreat' or a guided prolonged meditation. The other truth concerning alcohol is presented to us in the form of self-discovery: Westerners quickly come to an understanding they are terrible alcoholics and that their lack of awareness could make them the most difficult to rehabilitate.

And soon enough, they come to understand that meat is also a form of alcohol. He says these folks become disturbed by the quiet and peaceful gaze of an Indian who appears somewhat detached and elevated "above the situation." Even if he does not interpret that gaze as someone's standing above or beyond circumstance, Michaux says, the Westerner can never grasp it, figure it out. And soon enough the Westerner would figure that eating meat is bad and that his consumption is really bad for his own stomach as well as his other organs. Further along this line he will also forget about eggs (allegedly they increase aggression in man), he will learn how to sit, how to get up, how not to be critical, not overly defensive, etc.

Soon after this he will start fasting, remembering Mohammad's words that fasting is just an introduction, a door to religion, and he will continue living by the sheer will of his lungs which now work at their full capacity. He will use them like he was using his stomach before. He will start inhaling the air, free and clean, freed of any form and facial expression—which is an act both human and intimate: the air belongs to no one; it is at once nourishing and inoffensive to him. It is difficult to breathe the air in, then exhale, after it has entered all your chakras—your abdomen, your frontal region which stores white light, as it touches all our thoughts going further away to the region where there is nothing, an absolute void—devoid of any thought.

So, confronted with all this experience I imagine, it comes to me it must have been very difficult for the French to conquer Pondicherry. Out of all people on Earth the French strike me as utterly pompous, self-assured, "know-it-all folks"—it is often useless to give them any advice as they do not listen to any, and in this respect they may be even more hard-headed than the Brits, who were not really appreciated in this part of the Globe.

I had to inform the local population all the time "I am not French I come from that small country in Yugoslavia which favored Tito's and Nehru's friendship."

I should go back to Serbia before I spend all my money from Montmartre and before I waste all my health which once wasted and gone would not allow me, with or without any money, to move any further.

That thought was the only obsessive one which haunted me during my long New Year's meditation on the evening of December 31, 2014.

It seems it is a certain Tuesday; the days lose their frame and meaning... Perhaps it's Wednesday though, who would know?

And what's the Zen koan, and the moral drawn from

my journey to the deep Indian South? Here it comes:

In order to drink coconut milk you have to cut off almost half the coconut very fast. The movement has to be stable and rapid, and then only at that point you'd be able to get the sweetness of that milk. And so with our life, when we grow older and weary of it, we have to cut it off, throw the negative part out—so we can get deeper into something better.

****

When after this long watery promenade and sightseeing cruise we returned to our bungalow, I checked emails and was lit by a tiny virtual sun: my old pal Ljuba, who happened to be just nearby in Pondicherry, was getting ready to jump on a train and visit us here, in Kerala. He was such a sweet musician—perhaps the whole of next year will be—joyful and musical!

NEW YEAR'S EVENING, THE THIRD KARMIC DREAM

The celebration of New Year's 2015 arrived very calmly—a rather meditative experience heightened by Pierre's deep contemplation and that of his fellows who were meditating on the given theme "life without alcohol and how to survive without it." On the banks of the lake of that marshy Keralayeem, we met members of other unknown or barely known tourist groups who had just arrived. We share papaya salad with rice, and there is Rachel who all of a sudden decides to make a video with me. I introduce myself in Farsi and wish everyone a Happy New Year. Everyone becomes more and more jovial. They laugh, and some people play the sarod, a classical instrument which by the way is also a Sanskrit word for—music!

Some ladies dance with gardeners and waiters of the Keralayeem, some others voluptuously devour Indian pancakes made of rice-flour. Michelle was at it as well before she discovered there were cumin seeds, which she took for insects, so she screamed only to have it explained the seeds were not insects. This trip and this New Year's party was turning into some magnanimous lesson, a specific "guru experience", *gu* being the Sanskrit word for "teacher" and *ru*, the word signifying darkness. So a guru is the "person translating darkness into light," exactly what a teacher is supposed to do, that is, we were learning about our short and transient stay on Earth.

Everything went fine until someone exclaimed "midnight!" and everyone started lighting candles, cherry-bombs and fire-works which made a lot of noise and all of a sudden in my head I saw a battlefield, the recent bombing of Belgrade. See, memories are sly things—they never come to us as entire souvenirs when we want them, and then, whoops! They arrive abundantly we do not want them; they arrive at the moment when we want them the least, they arrive there to hurt us. At ten minutes after midnight I'm coming to an understanding this vicious noise is going to last for a while; the whole evening turns into a huge Munch painting, "the Scream." So here at the edge of the bush this noise neither comforts me nor scares me, it just returns me diabolically to when I was staring with my kid at the French TV for hours, a TV remote in one hand a telephone in the other, desperately trying to dial my family in Serbia, but all the phone lines cut off. I was not sure whether my mother was alive as well as all my not so near, and dearests.

Now I am completely swamped with memories which start whipping the back part of the brain where I hide my complete anxiety and pain. It was so stupid of Tito and Nehru to allow for that dreadful leak of consciousness in our sad, poor regions and on their inhabitants. I remembered the face of the Indian ambassador at some party in Paris, as well as his grim expression, while explaining to me the problem of Kosovo and then the one of Kashmir.

"You see," he said, "we have the same problem in fact: the masses of one's population in a fragile territory which does not belong to any particular country. I don't know exactly what Tito did with Kosovo, but Nehru made a terrible mistake when he brought to the floor that silly decision concerning Kashmir—he said that they should not be obliged to have birth control—so, now, I'm asking you, madam, is it normal we care more for the sacred cows than for people who live in that region?"

Now I felt entirely sick and ill at ease—once established, the painful thoughts and bad memories started taxing me, suffocating worse than a python or green cobra. I slowly stood and left our New Year's table. I kissed everyone good-bye, wishing them Happy New... and then back to my bungalow. I had the following dream that night:

I'm still young and as a correspondent to New York Arts magazine I happen to stand in front of the last installations of Joseph Beuys. He hasn't finished it so it is that "work in progress" which he himself entitled "Two aggregates of human being" and which presently (at least in my dream) is located on a grand podium of one of the Biennial's halls in Venice.

On the podium one can observe an inflated rubber

doll representing an American soldier. The doll has legs half-way buried into earth and above its head, that is, the entire space surrounding this doll, is stitched with cellophane which prevents the public from touching it. There is a plastic tube placed in the dolls mouth and the tube leads to a local water-fountain so that the public can "feed" the doll, if they deem it might be thirsty, etc. Next to this water fountain is another, with a tube to an opening in the doll's body we frequently call the "anus." Beuys himself stands in front of the fountains as he was commenting on his work of art:

"You see, a human being is a divided thing. Life circumstances disturb his equilibrium, be it in a war or in a car accident or a job which he does not like—there, he is likely to respond negatively. In fact, all we humans inhabit different realities that could only be called "human" if we mingle these realities into the big one. See, I'm pointing at the treasure box here which could be opened only with double and different keys."

A French sociologist standing next to me addresses Beuys personally: "You probably imply here a certain anti-realism. Feeling defends itself by preventing itself from observing something which is unbearable, thus replacing it immediately by a certain illusion."

"However, you must agree with me that the 'feeling' became immune from persuasion and the commercial propaganda imposed on it by that very man who creates perfect illusions but who does not accept the truth of a lie which reality feeds him. So even if you throw the man into jail or employ him to work at a degrading job he will still try to obtain a certain threshold of tolerance and be happy. You cannot strangle his hope for a better life just like that."

"Aha, but your installation does not show all this you've just mentioned—the doll's legs are stuck deep down in mud," exclaimed the sociologist.

"Oh but people are not dolls," Beuys jovially retorted.

"So why do you need to present us this installation with the doll?," the sociologist asked seriously.

"Well, I did so in order to better explain the phenomenon of "anti-realism of feeling," Beuys replied, as he was a great artist, but also a great player and a great voyager of his time.

If we remember Benjamin's notion of time(s) and his description of the world in it, we will remember that he conceived a "player" as someone who liked to spend his time leisurely. On the contrary, a "voyager" to him represented a person who was able to accumulate time and subsequently get charged and emptied of it, like a battery. The third of Benjamin's categories was "patience" which was supposed to return us to the past and this category was represented best by the notion of cinema or cinematography. The 'player' sits nervously in a movie house trying to fast-forward time; he would wait his turn impatiently as he wants to be the winner. His brother, the "voyager," desperately tries to slow the moment down as he lives from one moment to another contemplating the value of that time. He is eager to prolong his momentum into infinity, like we often do in childhood, whereas patience as a category is not concerned with the multiplicity of meanings with which the voyager likes to endow his time. Patience is never rushed and as a category it readily waits for its moment to pop out of the given combination. The notion of film, of cinema, is born exactly due to this at once leisurely and busy research, executed in the category of patience. Thus we have the whole history of cinematography which disappears and then comes back to us again so that it can be reinvented in some other form and category, etc.

But am I dreaming all this, or am I really in a certain film, more precisely, am I in a film where I'm having a dream about cinematography, I wondered. The green field of the Venetian island of Lido changed quickly into the landscape of yet another Biennial pavilion where our very own Marina Abramovic was washing ox bones in front of a large audience. It's the pavilion of ex-Yugoslavia, where the story of subsequent civil wars mingle with the stories of the killing of the population, torture and mutilation and all this repeated every ten minutes on the screen in an endless loop. In front of this pavilion I could see clearly a tiny figure dressed in very bright colors—yellow, purple and green; yes, it was the venerable Lama Tenzin in person, who came here to encourage his disciple, Marina, to boost her with additional courage and energy, I gathered. I was just about to bow to him and start my habitual prostrations in front of such a high priest when he waved his hand all the way up, smiling benevolently at me. As his smile had the nuance of a real, non-preconceived emotion and an expression not usually to be found with the representatives of the highest Buddhist clergy, I happily jumped over the fresh lawn and pranced in his direction.

"Oh, that's you, our dear and venerable Rinpoche," I exclaimed, still shocked by this unexpected encounter. This dream was becoming a really great film I did not want to end—"and you know, I was really looking for you for a long time, ever since we said good-bye at your residence in Massachusetts, I haven't stopped thinking of you! Do you still reside in the U.S.?" I launched my naive inquiries.

"Oh, yes and no," he responded, "but to answer your question in a more precise way I should tell you that I am here, in this space—ALL OVER the place." As he was saying these words to me, he used his hands to make an all-encompassing *Gyan mudra,* which was to summarize and round up the entire universe while showering benefits and well-being onto those bathing nearby in his divine presence.

"Ohh! And I missed you so much!! And I looked for you everywhere and wanted to write to you—but what can a poor human do? So imperfect, so dumb, always running after some earthly "affair," wasting his own time, inventing obligations for himself and for others, before s/he gets lost, like an insect, yes, entirely lost, as s/he understands at one point or another that s/he is just tending to that stupid *samsara* which is there to devour them in return! It seems I haven't listened to your instructions carefully, it feels... as if I threw your precious advice into the Seine, a river flowing through the city of Paris, where I resided for a moment."

"And what is there now that you think you should hear from me and that has escaped you so far?" asked the teacher, in his infinite patience and tenderness. "I always said… and I will tell you one more time: you have to meditate more, to practice mantras, read *nondro* in the morning and before going to bed—you should be calming your spirit, not only your body; you should contemplate the Great Void in the afternoon, as much as I do and many other people." There was a spark of a sudden understanding in his eye, lit up because of my particular case, I thought, as he stopped his light contemplation and all of a sudden asked a jovial question: "Is there a cafe or a tea house nearby? We could have some tea, in fact—and you could dance for me to show how happy you truly are!"

I started laughing—this such unusually usual and somewhat vulgar request coming from such a high Tibetan priest seemed to me like a fairy tale within a script of this Venetian art movie in which I participated for truly professional reasons. We went to a small motel which was down the road although its entrance halls resounded with terrible noise from all the Italian TV channels. Football fans were quite unhappy with the development of an important match and in a really loud manner they were letting everyone know their feelings.

"Let us have tea here, in the room which I have booked for tonight," with a serious voice the Lama exclaimed, "as I think I should give you my last instructions in this lifetime, you know, we are likely to meet again, but not so soon, certainly not before our fourth and future lifetime!"

I followed him down the corridor which became suddenly lit by an unusual golden light. His room looked more like a small Buddhist temple than a motel room—there was no bed in its middle but a golden *stupa* instead, and a chair which was turned for the occasion into the Lama's decorated throne. Several *termas,* sacred books containing the teachings following the lineage of the Lama's karmic family, lay spread open, as well as the precise Buddhist transmissions/instructions which the spiritual teachers bestowed from one generation to another.

"No, you don't have to dance," the venerable Rinpoche decided, "although in all your previous lives you used to be a renowned dancer. I want to explain to you the principle of vacuity, the great VOID, which some people call the primordial mover of all existence and some call universe. Take off all your clothes, now you don't really need them."

He embraced me lightly and lifted me up, only to place me like a precious parcel at the altar of the golden stupa. As I was transforming slowly into that plastic doll from the Joseph Beuys installation I was becoming petrified at the sudden change of events... then we made love, if one could call this entirely non-erotic act "love-making" or sex! While he was at it, my guru was reciting incessantly the great Samantabhadra's 100 syllable mantra:

oṃ vajrasattva samaya/manupālaya/vajrasattva tvenopa tiṣṭha dṛḍho me bhava/sutoṣyo me bhava/supoṣyo me bhava/anurakto me bhava sarva siddhiṃ me prayaccha/ sarva karma su ca me/cittaṃ śreyaḥ kuru hūṃ/ ha ha ha ha hoḥ/bhagavan /sarva tathāgata vajra/mā me muñca vajrī bhava mahā samaya sattva aḥ

At the end of his recitation he added in English "this is all void, nothingness," and then "you see, there's nothing special in all of this as neither you nor I are really here but we are all minuscule parts of great NOTHINGNESS."

Resembling pretty much Beuys's doll, I kept repeating mechanically after him all the parts of the mantra. In the end, one would hope that I gathered as well the quintessence of the meaning of the Absolute.

Then all of a sudden, this film was over and I could hear the ending of the film and the noise of the film's projector.

In my Indian bungalow I suddenly realized the noise was actually coming from the mosquitoes who claimed here their absolute damp and humid territory. I opened the bungalow's door wide. It was getting bright and sunny. It was the first day of our Christian year 2015.

SHIVA'S TEMPLE IN VAIKOM

After a very meager breakfast we set out to Vaikom to see Shiva's great Mahadeva temple. The huge divided courtyard led to several buildings and as such, came the closest to the notion of a big undivided space that resembled the universe dotted with stars—only here we had candles turned on and off. In this temple like in all others there was the prevailing smell of incense and music floating through the oily air. Hindus like to decorate their houses with endless details, especially their most sacred house. A temple like this gets to be adorned with numerous light and ephemeral elements which get close to the invisible world and far from the notion of the Real. The temple surely belonged to the people who were closest to the Absolute, to the radically religious. So contrary to us "Westerners," Hindus entered their temple to gain strength and not develop the feeling of helplessness before their God(s). In this same spirit the very prayer and meditation which goes with it are only spiritual exercises to them, as can be found in drawings at Kali's altar. It's interesting to notice the entrances to smaller temples within the big complex magnanimously built but the interior of these temples are ridiculously tiny, sometimes built only as a niche or single altar. Our guide is beautiful Natalie, renamed Laxmi, a French girl born to French parents here in Kerala. Her parents went on one of these long holidays as tourists, then smitten by the beauty of India, they never desired to return home. She took us through the entrance where you take off shoes then turn cameras off, then through the maze of interspersed buildings, rooms and corridors, connected or divided by inner ponds/lakes, through the entire complex of temples which seemed endless.

However, our "temple-seeing" had its end: a sumptuous lunch to which we were all invited by Natalie and her parents, in their home turned into a real Indian household. There on the mats stretched right on the floor she served us lunch. The plates were just green banana leaves on which we placed our choice of assorted foods, chunks of something—I forgot the names…

The temple itself consisted of a few rooms flowing one into another, like a river, and the last room literally gave way to a lake. In each of these rooms were small groups of musicians playing ragas, or these early morning prayers which would awaken consciousness? They were capable of enlarging the spirit as they were quite magical, quite powerful in mastering clarity in a subject. Or they would play violent afternoon prayers on their fiery instruments. These invited action and growth of one's fortune. Then they would play evening prayers to call families to gather and pay tribute to the gods such as Shiva, Parvati and Ganesha, who in turn would be invited to sit at table. The evening odes were played on the instrument *nagaswaram*, the long wind instrument which hypnotizes snakes. But then from each room we could hear a choir singing the magical triangular AUM. I think they sang the Vedas, more precisely the verses from the Upanishads, as well as those from the Tantra of the Great Liberation.

These hymns celebrated the union of the individual with the Absolute, as they worshiped the mastering of spirit over body, they were spiritually charged, victorious as they literally spat over the defeated daemons, those inner as well as the external ones. Here lived Jayadeva, a poet in the twelfth century who endowed these hymns with his own style and tradition, and his verse even got inscribed in the marble steps of the temple. They call his interpreting style in poetry and music *sopana sangeetham*.

Around 6pm, when the sun goes down, we hear from all over, especially from villages and the countryside where one hears everything with greater distinction, the blaring of sea shells announcing the hour of prayer. Everyone, except those from the pariah caste have to enter their temples to join their own wooden pagodas or those made in bamboo or stone. The Hindus first start singing in their temples, they pray and then start throwing themselves to the ground—Shiva himself has entered their bodies, or perhaps Kali or some other deity. The majority of the believers are simple hardworking people who have mastered this or that spiritual practice, and reaching this or that level, there they wallow, meaning: they never advance or move forward.

According to Michaux, these are "good soldier Schweiks", they never dare laugh or cry, and above all they never allow Europeans to watch them pray. I think that Michaux was an exception, he saw them pray, and so did I—but one thing is sure, at the end of their prayer they say "today I have accomplished a very tiny bit of a reunion with the Absolute".

The highest Hindu ecstasy however is not to be identified with Christian mystical ecstasy—and Saint Angela and Saint Francis of Assisi as much as St Teresa d'Avila, do not reach God through a sort of ecstasy which leaves them naked, annulled and devastated. Religion as such is very important for both parties. If we remember the Christian churches and cathedrals—we see in front of them as in front of the Hindu temples, long rows of beggars waiting for you to throw a coin into their cup. We know a story of a woman who was frequenting Shiva's temple for years asking Shiva constantly to return her dead husband to her. Her husband promised one hundred children to this poor lady but he made only eighteen and then he died. As in India the widows cannot get remarried, she was stubbornly coming to the temple and praying to Shiva to return her dead husband. She knew no other man could give her children as she realized having children was the cause and consequence of her going to bed with her husband—this much this poor woman gathered in her life.

The Hindus steadily believe the gods themselves reincarnate into humans as much as they believe in human reincarnation. Every fifteen years there is a deity reincarnated into a human, and Vishnu can reincarnate twelve successive times into different babies. That's why Indians often think they have gods in their family—the parents hope a god will reincarnate into their sons, and girls hope these reincarnations will show up and marry them. Their prayers, or *shaktas*, if we were to translate them, would sound as the most banal and vulgar prayers, where the believers demand the most trivial favors from the gods—"Hey, dude, are you gonna help me or drop me?" sort of demands.

However, Shiva is not the only deity, although he's the supreme in that pantheon—with a million avatars or manifestations but the most famous has always been Krisna, Krsna or Christ.

If you ask a Hindu from the South of India what are the names of the gods who decorate numerous reliefs (*gopuram*) he will say "Oh boy, there are so many of them—how do I know!"

What's interesting to me is that the reliefs contain the respectful, nicely carved images of the deities who the Hindus adore, and also those who they abhor. This is perhaps the major difference between our Western pantheon and theirs. When a Christian presents an image of Satan, he is not going to paint him in respectful and joyful colors, but our Hindu brothers are going to do just the opposite—they're going to present Evil with respect in order to pacify it. If we carefully study Ramayana, we will discover that two thirds of the manuscript is devoted to some asshole deities and their evil undoing, and that the last third describes the essence of their black magic activities. Those demons, so-called inferior deities, and evil spirits spend their time contriving and organizing wars whereas good gods are often so busy trying to help people in distress that they are not able to control or vanquish the demons. So where do Hindus draw the line dividing gods from the ordinary people? The gods possess magic power which people do not have in order to pursue their evil human deeds.

Hindus revel in their psychic powers. The power should dominate the personality—so a man who can curse a neighbor with success is held in great esteem as he is considered a special being. One of the greatest Hindu as well as Buddhist saints, Milarepa, started exercising his telepathic powers as a boy. He practiced black magic to burn the stables and crops of his neighbors, age eleven, and he also reveled in sending wild animals to kill them. Then later, as he grew up, he regretted his evil deeds and tried to compensate for them. Anyhow, his soliloquy in expressing deep sorrow for those past deeds is considered one of the most beautiful pages of classic literature in Sanskrit.

One thing that caught my attention in front of this particular temple were the big scales placed in front of all the separate entrances to the temple, and these apertures were separated by golden *stupas*. When I asked Laxmi, our gentle guide, the purpose of these scales perched there, she said the scales served to weigh babies as well as their mothers, their total weight to be given as a special gift to Shiva just after a baby was born. When she noticed how shocked I was on hearing her words she laughed out loud and explained to me that the weight offering here was truly symbolic and human sacrifice was in reality quite unknown in this region. She did not convince me. She tried to divert the conversation quickly by inviting everyone to enter the temple's interior: "Come in to see the altars and the thousands of oil lamps which give light to the temple, and there are hundreds of musicians here about to start to play their prayers as the Bhakti cult is still very big here."

We came in and the strong perfumes of some hundreds of incense sticks hit us as we walked. When I was a kid, I remember we were buying these sticks made of patchouli and jasmine powders but these new perfumes that reigned in the temple I had never smelled before.

I was still thinking of those scales and of human sacrifice offered to their gods. Hindus are well known to be faithful to their idea of making all sorts of offerings—so if they offer a goat to Shiva's altar that means they are poor and have nothing better to offer. Some time ago there was a caste in India whose unique task was to look for human sacrifice and in such a role they traveled through the country. They would find some ignorant traveler and quickly cut off his head with a sword, no one could hear his complaint, and their almighty god—who understands and forgives everyone's action, would approve of their unreasonable and terrible offering. So they would continue their murky wanderings, on the look-out for new victims that included in the period of the last two centuries mostly American and European tourists. There were also some Australians in this crowd, although these were famous for escaping such a dreadful fate as they had some rebellious local tribes of aborigines at home who made them both cautious and afraid in traveling through unknown lands. In general, whenever such nomadic travelers visiting India stopped sending postcards to their families in Europe, or wherever they came from, the Hindus claimed to know where these missing people disappeared to in their country. They were certain these poor creatures fell victim to the religious ecstasy of their blood-thirsty sects. However, they really did not try hard to locate the missing victims with the local police and they would soon afterwards forget these sad cases.

I stayed for a long time in this temple; however, I always kept an eye on my fellow-travelers so they could not say that I was the one who really intended to get lost. I swear to you though I really wanted to get lost in there. I have attended many concerts of Indian music in my past, at least they were as numerous as those discs I bought in assorted shops in the U.S. and in Europe, but I have never heard such fantastic heavenly music as I was hearing at this moment in this particular temple! And these were just simple believers who probably had no pretensions to call themselves musicians. They spontaneously gathered here and were playing the evening ragas. If not better than Nishat Kahn, Zakir Hussein or Ustad Vilayat Khan—then certainly with more *bhava*, zest or inspiration rising above any of these famous musicians. I swear they sounded better than the renowned Ustad Sukhvinder Singh, and more sublime than Nikhil Banerjee or Laxmi Shankar... perhaps they were even better than the unforgettable Ravi Shankar, although I could not claim any degree of excellence surpassing this last one.

RENAN, OUR TEACHER

Renan is truly a very spiritual person, a real Hindu in that regard. He was born to a very rich aristocratic family in France, but he set out on his own rejecting everything material and materialistic in his way (and he had so much stuff to throw out, indeed!) At one point, before I got to know him better, I thought he belonged to the group of silly Western fashionistas who buy Hindu spirituality the way the West buys stuff all the time from the indigenous Orientals—they buy tranquility, medical herbs and healthy food from the indigenous to make a profit and a fetish out of any spirituality. We have a number of examples of that sort and it seems the American Indians and the Latino Americans, including the Brazilian peoples, pay the highest tribute to that trend. However, I was wrong in regards Renan's character. On this journey he proved to be more than coherent in following his mission. He entered the temple twice that particular morning. And while others were buying funny souvenirs, he was reading the *Bhagavad Gita*, then collecting statues of Buddha, and he was happy like a new born child anytime he would hear a melody, raga or a hymn coming from the temple. All in all, one could clearly see his heart was anchored in this land. And later, as we were performing heavy ashtanga exercises under his awakened supervision, he was simultaneously reading parts of the *Bhagavad Gita* to us.

The most interesting story in it was the one in which the great warrior, Arjuna, middle aged and quite confused, in *mezzo camino della sua vita*, gets into a spiritual and existential crisis and begs Krisna, his spiritual leader, to drive his chariot as the former is so depressed that he can't even do that. Krisna retorts "please remain in your caste of *shatriya* as you are likely to perform all other jobs the gods have endowed you with, worse than this one. Your heart has closed to it temporarily, but even if you continue doing your work with half an effort you'll be doing it much better than any new work you want to choose right now."

I have often thought, when exhausted from this path I've chosen, where is Krisna to manifest right now? And I had my answer soon enough. Renan and Laxmi took us to a promised lunch soon after the sight-seeing, and after we were to watch the three- hour preparatory exercises for a rehearsal of a Kathakali theater where Laxmi had a leading role.

Kathakali, an original mixture of songs and movement, was created 1500 years ago, just here in Kerala in the south of India. At first they were dances performed to celebrate the Bhagavati cult and they were performed during those religious festivals where the performers wore elaborate masks and colorful costumes which do not fully hide the impeccably made-up actors. Although Kathakali includes several socio-religious dances such as *Sastrakhali* and *Ezamatukali*, the most popular is *Ashtapadi atom* from Yajadeva's Geeta Govinda. This is a story about Krisna, dressed as a modest cowboy, his Radha, and three other cowgirls.

In the 17th century, Manidevan or Sri Samuthiri Maharajah of Kozhikode wrote the *Krisnageeta*, a choreo-play to be performed on eight consecutive nights, containing special ritual plays written in Sanskrit. The performance of *Krisnanattam* was strictly reserved for the monks of the Guruvayur temple as well as members of the Samuthiri royal family. *Krisnanattam* told stories from Krisna's life through dance and pantomime, and the narrative part was performed by the musicians.

According to legend, the great maharajah of Kottarakkara (an ex-province of Kerala), being himself a passionate patron of all traditional arts, had invited his Majesty, the maharajah of Samuthiri, to watch the performance of *Krisnanattam* in Kottarakkara. The maharajah of Samuthiri refused his invitation, explaining that *Krisnanattam* was not meant to be performed for the simple and banal audience of South Kerala. In order to make the maharajah change his mind, Kottarakkara Tampuran wrote several plays entitled *Ramanattam* (performance of Rama) which were also to be performed on eight consecutive nights. In the beginning, *Ramanattam* told the stories of Ramayana, but in time it became a choreo-dramatic form of Kathakali and included many other traditional stories.

So Kathakali had united the elements taken from

Krisnanattam and *Ramanattam,* but subsequently included some other elements from local folklore and the warriors' dances from Kerala. As a result, it was very popular—a people's theatre for people. The performances were performed in local Malayalam (a mix of Sanskrit and Tamil languages, also called Manipravalam). The people of this province started going more regularly to the theater, as they previously could not understand anything in Sanskrit, a language reserved for the privileged. After a while they also got rid of the masks in this theatre and replaced them with a very elaborate make-up. The actors were obliged to spend several hours before each performance applying make-up. We got a taste of this elaborate process during the three hours it took to prepare the performance—they were in no hurry, slowly putting on their make-up.

In the 17th century, acting was separate from singing, which facilitated the actors' concentration on dramatic expression. By the end of the 17th century facial emotion was given central interest in the play. In order to enhance it the actors color their faces with white chalk or green paste and the emotional reaction is underlined with a red line. In the 18th century, the Kathakali show assumed its final shape, staged the way we see it today; the role of the timpani was emphasized and the animal noises and so-called demons were quite diminished. Mudras were introduced into the performance and the entire corporal expression was harmonized, but the most important change perhaps was the final depiction of *five character types* represented through their three-dimensional make-up. The unforgettable character kati (knife) who is a mixture of an elegant dandy and a perfect knave, becomes the leading role in Kathakali.

Kathakali were traditionally performed during the religious festivals, but today's performance, such as we see, is only four decades old. Nowadays the show is not tied to temples or king's palaces, but the performance of this theater is always connected to some holiday or special event.

I adored Kathakali, like any other hybrid form of art, and I even tried to introduce it in a play we did with the Living Theater. However, the duration of the show is endlessly prolonged here in India, or should we say, rather shortened in the West?

Originally there were 101 stories in Kathakali, but as the performance of each was supposed to last a whole night, there were only around thirty plays which were able to be staged. However, today's plays last only three to four hours, which means only fragments of the shorter stories are being staged. Although Kathakali is represented in its classical form, entire innovations are welcomed because its character is always scenic and abstract, which goes with the music of the given period. Some of the traditional stories performed nowadays include *Kiratham* (which is a story of Arjuna's fight with the lord Shiva) and *Karnashapatam*, both taken from *Mahabharata*.

I would like to see them all, but how and when? Particularly now that the curtain of globalization has fallen on almost all theaters in the world. I see even here they have started showing Shakespeare's *King Lear*, Homer's *Iliad* and Goethe's *Faust* each in their Kathakali version, indeed.

The language in which Kathakali plays were written is *Manipravalam*. Although most of the poems were set to *ragas* rooted in the microtonal Carnatic Indian music, there is also a style of special, pure notes, the *Sopanam*. This style, typical of the Kerala region, comes from songs performed at temples at the times when the Kathakali plays were first staged. As in the acting, the music performed in Kathakali has two variations, the Northern and Southern. The so-called Northern style was developed by the Kalamandalam from Kerala and appeared only in the 20th century. The Southern, or rather melancholic style, was developed by musicians such as Selvaganesh and Mahadevan.

Kathakali plays are usually performed in front of a huge lamp, Kalivilakku (*kali* means to play, and *vilakku*, a lamp). That is, if we can call a basket made of thick reed and dumped into coconut oil a lamp. Once upon a time, such an object was the only source of light in temples, palaces and the houses of aristocrats—at least during the times of the performance. This one was always followed by musical accompaniment (*geetha*) on the appropriate instruments (*vadya*). The most popular instruments were percussion instruments, known as *chenda* and *maddalam*. There were always two singers—the leading voice is *ponani,* always followed by *singidi.* The leading singer was the first to hit *chengila* (metal gong with a stick), but unlike our Western performances, the actors here would not pronounce a single word. They were only communicating with their hands, facial expressions and through a rhythmical dance which replaces dialogue most of the time, except on the rare occasion when an actor utters a word (in intervals of every hour or so).

A Kathakali actor is extremely focused, has great physical stamina and exercises great patience—but then you will say "and what actor is not made that way?" True, but these here gain such qualities through long training in a Martial art originating in Kerala which makes them extremely fit for this sort of acting. Their rehearsals last sometimes between eight and ten hours and are rather ferocious.

In a Kathakali play the major focus is on hands as each of their gestures (mudras) carries a specific meaning. Also the facial expression (rasa) is very important in a play, as well as the entire movement of the actor's body.

The facial expressions are also called "emotional exercises" and we had the good fortune to observe them in detail during the long preparation of our generous hosts/actors before their show. The expressions are rooted in the study of *Natya Shastra*, a compendium on acting and performing arts which emerged from several centuries of theatrical practice by hereditary actors, passing their tradition orally from generation to generation (the compilation was first recorded in 200 BC). The science of expression divides these into nine categories, which in their turn subdivide into all other classical Indian art forms. The actors spend hours and hours studying special exercises which help them control eye-movements, which are of extreme importance in this tradition.

There are twenty-four basic mudras. However, with the permutation and combining of different movements they created a certain system of moving their hands in a play, and contemporary actors are keen to follow this style. The mudras are divided into two groups—*samaanas* where you move only one hand to form mudras, and *misra* mudras where you make forms with both hands. They are a sort of semantic that serves actors to tell a story in pantomime. The basic facial expression of an actor is called "navarasam" (*navarasas* is the term for "nine tastes," which we would translate as nine emotions or sentiments). These sentiments include *sringaram* (love, affection), *hasiyam* (mockery, irony), *bayanakam* (fear), *karunam* (pathos), *roudram* (anger, fit) *veeram* (courage), *beebhatsam* (disgust), *albhutam* (confusion, surprise) and *shantam* (peace, tranquility).

One of the most interesting elements in Kathakali is the make-up codex. The actors divide their make up into five basic shades which are called *pachca, Kathi, kari, taadi,* and *minuku.* Pachca, or green, is applied to an actor whose role is dignified but wicked. These *rajasick* characters, as they call them, are real anti-heroes in a play. However, the really evil set of characters called the *Blackbeards* are always covered with either red or black make-up. The women and the ascetics are depicted in bright yellow, while minor gods such as Hanuman (monkey god) and lord Shiva are represented in white.

The spectacle that we were supposed to watch was in fact taken from the first act of the *Mahabharata,* where Shiva and his major consort, Parvati, try to have negotiations. In the end of this act, our gracious hostess, Laxmi, in the role of Parvati, danced a sublime Tamil dance for us, and that dance, called *barathanatyam* totally revitalized me.

I was asleep in my existential slumber, when all I had to do was go back to theater. The very next morning I got so inspired I performed 108 yogin's salutations, which were very physically strenuous. I did not utter a single sigh or complaint, worthy of any Living Theater member and all the present yoga participants. Renan's students applauded at the end. They congratulated me on such enthusiasm and we all walked together merrily to the beach. The sunset seemed really perfect.

The Raven

(after E.A. Poe)

And it does not mean that
all the things won't return with their dreadful refrain 'never more',
remember René Char who said "everything that was
taken was returned to him, even his little red truck,"
but what it means is they won't come back with that crazy, insane—
but to me so dear, adorable in-ten-si-ty;

Oh, your pupil, raven, glistening in your oily eye-
shows you at your best, the perfect, arrogant and abusive creature,
domineering; your shape of a lonely bird—foreboding,
your eye, translucent and penetrating, observes me intensely
just this morning, as you land on my Kerala terrace,
yes you do and then take fruits from my palm, I've just cut it
for you, and as you gobble these pieces from my hand,
I hear myself whispering semi-absently
"never more", "never more"...

This poem I wrote one sunny afternoon while staring into the tree-tops, sitting on "our" veranda. All of a sudden, a shiny feathery black raven landed straight from a tree-top onto our table. He looked at me with curiosity then started turning his head from left to right, exactly as his brothers the Hindus usually do. They neither negate nor confirm any given situation. And when I began throwing pieces of fruit to him he hopped quickly to me, placing his open beak next to my left hand (he must have been doing it all the time with other Keralayeem guests). He carefully picked a slice of banana from my palm and took an equally sudden flight back. So our hopes and expectations equally go away fast, I thought. By now it was becoming clear that Rachel-Shirin and I would never visit our Zoroastrian village—at least it was not meant to happen this time around.

As the days rolled by this modest girl was slowly but surely turning into a spoiled and capricious grand *banu* from Northern Iran, whose mouth cannot be assuaged for a second—as soon as she would open it imperative orders would fly out. However, as three quarters of our fellow-passengers did not show any response to her infantile questions and expectations, she began to be seriously annoyed, avoiding common meals, dinners, the walks they pursued together. True, our group made up of petty French bourgeoisie making racist sneers did not look any better than her. Rachel comes from a general's family. Her father was a general pilot himself from a wealthy Iranian family. At the time she studied psychology in Paris. I think just to make her own life a little bit more bearable and her thoughts a bit less oppressive. She obtained an incredibly maniacal paranoia when her I-phone charger burnt up and, to top it off, a night moth flew into our bungalow. She withdrew to the bathroom, divided only by a simple reed wall from the huge jungle surrounding us, and there she stayed for hours howling out loud : "It is here, it is getting ready to bite me!"

She cried like this the whole night long as her worst fear, probably dating from her childhood, was someone was going to rape her or pierce her body with a phallic object—or both. The pillow was her *transitional object* so she constantly trailed a cushion behind her. Otherwise we got along well.

I barely managed to fall asleep that evening and when I finally did I had my last Karmic dream. After this I could not even tell feverish reality from my nightmarish frame of mind in high fever.

In the dream I sat in a huge baobab tree in front of Beau's and my house, in Kaduna, northern Nigeria, when all of a sudden a funny little black guy, our gardener Christopher, showed up. The little Nigerian boy held in one hand a huge bowl with the water still boiling inside and in that water a mighty mix of different herbal medicines, salts and stones he did not fail to place fast under my nose. "Small madam, (*he always called me "small madam" and Beau's mother "big madam"*), you are very ill, drink this quickly so you feel better." I didn't always trust Christopher's words as he changed his mind quickly, but as he was here on the edge of the African bush, my absolute guide through the "zone" and my friend, I decided perhaps the only thing to do was to swallow that awful concoction. This way I showed my absolute trust—the thing was we were in Nigeria, the country that gained its independence from British colonial rule just a few months before our arrival; however, the local population still cringed even talking to white people, let alone giving them any helping hand. Christo took care of our garden, cleaned it from pythons which were regular in the bush, picking those huge mango fruits fallen from surrounding trees as these mangoes were attracting *tse-tse* flies, the reason Europeans called Nigeria "the graveyard of white settlers." On top of all other services Christopher tried with great zeal to teach me Hausa language, so that I could feel more at home.

I drank his liquid and soon enough I noticed I was shaking with some strange flu—the cold waves of sweat soon replaced by waves of terrible, hot temperature—I felt weak like a little girl. I entered the house and lay down, but my bed was shaking with me. I was all in shivers and the strongest malaria fever shook both my bed and my body. I was almost unconscious when I woke and saw Beau's extremely serious face above my pillow. He was worried and probably been there for a while. Christo perched his head behind him, also visibly worried. "Call quickly for the doctor," Beau snapped at Christopher, and those were the last words I heard that day.

I woke now covered with a gluey, sticky cold sweat. All the bed covers wet and my bungalow bed shaking like that one in Africa, and I shook my body in it, in that bungalow, which was still terribly dark. My first thought was to wake Rachel, ask her to bring me some water, but she mustered her courage, left the bathroom and the ominous insect, and had gone to seek help on her own. It was almost noon when our twelve fellow travelers began visiting our bungalow one by one. They would stop by my bed and stare helplessly—asking me how I felt and if I needed any immediate help. True, now I remember—that very evening preceding the horrible night, I felt a tremor and terrible pain in all my muscles and bones, and tried to ignore physical discomfort as a good yogini, and tried to enjoy one of my last beautiful sunsets in Keralayeem. By now it was more than certain neither the vaccine I received against malaria in Paris nor all those dreadful bitter pills I was swallowing daily had any effect on me.

I was sincerely hoping I had not caught the deadliest malaria this time, certain *Plasmodium falciparum* said to be resistant to all worldly medicament. According to the World Health organization this type of malaria was wide-spread in India because of the Ganges, polluted daily by all sorts of organic and inorganic trash. For three thousand years the Hindus have been constantly burning their dead and throwing their dead, and not entirely burnt bodies into the river. Still, until recently the Ganges was relatively biologically preserved and flowing. But the constant influx of cadavers combined with other recent techno junk had finally breached its lagoons, leaving the infectious steady water to flood its banks, and above this immobile watery mass clouds of mosquitoes buzzed their short lives away. These guys transmit malaria, Dengue or chikungunya to humans—and mind you, just the mention of these maladies' names can cause the disintegration of pages which then fall from the medical dictionary in which they are written. No, I'm just kidding, but the new president of India himself scorned his people quoting the fact that 600 million of them still do not use proper English toilets as they ease themselves in the river. He begged them to return dignity to their country, recently criticized by the United Nations, which exposed the fact that around forty-five percent of the population was using mobile telephones while only thirty-one percent were using toilets.

Soon enough, Renan came back to our bungalow, and this time he brought two masseuses who literally submerged my body into a tub filled with aromatic oils from bottom to top; then they began to massage me quickly. This action lasted hours so by 4 pm I felt a sudden relief. I was even ready to jump on my feet and say good-bye to this environment, this wild ocean, the temples and the bush surrounding them, all of which was simply Kerala to me. I went to the beach where a strong wind was creating tall spiral dunes which in turn began to cover with fine grayish sand those rare tourists who, despite the sudden change of climate, still remained. The ocean was unusually calm, not a single trace of the smallest wave. It was flat "as a sheet of metal," as the Turks would say. I dunked my feet, and just as I was getting ready to pick up a small shell, a huge wave appeared in front of me. It literally emerged from beneath my feet, then with mad speed lifted and dragged me almost ten feet down towards the left side of the beach. I got up with difficulty but I heard voices running behind me—they were trying to help and rescue me. A young Canadian couple who happened to be there ran towards me asking if I needed any help. Yes, of course, I needed help—the ocean robbed me of my glasses and I could not see a single thing in front of me in that landscape. I was repeating to them endlessly how I managed to figure the secret of the Tsunami—that it would come from nowhere, a tectonic monster would swallow anything on its way. It would vacuum and devour not only people and their houses and animals on its way, but also swallow the beach, its surrounding landscapes without a trace of warning.

Now it was my first real encounter with India, but on that particular day there was yet another. The Canadians walked me to the exit of the beach where the road was visible, where the rickshaw drivers waited for the tourists to take them back to the hotel. I really still felt quite feverish but the thought that our journey, racing to its end, convinced me I should not go straight to the hotel but instead try to see Shiva's temple in Alleppey just one more time.

KRISNA'S TEMPLE in ALLEPPEY or a MAHADEVA'S ADVENTURE?

I told the first rickshaw driver I ran into to take me quickly to *Keralayeem* where we would stop for exactly three minutes (so I could take the other pair of glasses from my suitcase), then continue to Alleppey. The thin dry Indian looked at me in surprise and with the usual "namaskar, namaste" asked me for my name and where I was from. Dryly, with an answer, I was curious to know how much this trip would cost me. The man, whose name was Belesh, also replied dryly, in a cold unpleasant tone "1800 rupees."

"But wait," I said, "it cost only 500 going to the farthest beach in Keralayeem!"

"Yes," the man simply replied, "but I could take the lady who… lives only for Art and from her arts to the biggest and best Krisna temple in South India. And I am on my way there to make my evening prayer."

"How do you know, Belesh, I do not only live *for* Art but I live *from* it as well?" I asked, quite confused, as I was dressed in the most conservative teacher's clothing there was nothing artistic in my image.

"Oh I know many, many things," he said in a deep voice.

After a short negotiation he dropped his price to 600 rupees and we set out on our journey—which lasted hours. During the entire trip Belesh kept stopping his rickshaw, buying and drinking water, stopping by road altars along the main road leading to the temple, then he would place the Indian red powder, *bindi,* on my brow in order to protect both of us, I guess, from an evil eye.

"Hey, where are we now?" I exclaimed after two hours of his driving, having realized every landscape around us resembled a region geographically different from the state of Kerala.

We were crossing an industrial zone filled with advertising boards, images of the latest mobile telephones and numerous local mosques.

"Don't worry," he said, noticing by my face that I was afraid of having launched into an exaggerated adventure, "in only half an hour—not more than thirty minutes we will reach Mahadeva's temple!"

The temple we reached was enormous, perhaps too big to fit a religious dream. It appeared more like a shopping mall or any *suk*, abundant market of North Africa; or it was more like an old Russian-Jewish market, a bazaar consisting of numerous buildings put together under the same glass roof, like I saw once in Moscow or Odessa—yes, it was all that and at the same time it wasn't anything I had ever seen before. This building, of exceptional architecture and size, was lit by zillions of oil lamps neatly placed in their respective niches. Was the real function of these lamps to light up the believer's mind definitively bringing it to the clearest plane called "pure enlightenment?" I dared not ask.

The very entrance to the temple was 500 meters and along its corridors I found everything I ever wanted to find in India: incense, Krisna posters, music discs with Ganesha's mantras, silk cushions, spices, Buddha statues in bronze and red powder to apply *bindi* which Belesh had recently placed on my third eye.

He didn't do that out of amusement or for the sake of having fun, as I first thought, but to make me blend into the enormous crowd which filled the cobbled courtyard of the temple. In this crowd there was not a single European, all were local people, equally tired and dry as our friend Belesh, who suddenly disappeared right in front of me as he probably went to pray. All these people were the heart of the real working class of India who came to this temple to pray after a long day of work. But then I made a terrible mistake—there was a huge banyan tree in the middle of the temple's courtyard (as tall as that legendary banyan tree which hid Buddha in its deep curves); inadvertently, I took out my camera and I was not even sure I wanted to take a photo.

"Please, just put back that object into your bag," an angry local hissed at me and I instinctively felt there was not a trace of polite request in his command. It was a real order that sounded rather menacing, so I quickly hid my camera and modestly lit an incense instead.

"Oh yes, I am sorry Krisna, sorry Radha"—I quietly murmured, then again, "I am sorry Christ, I am sorry Buddha, Mahomet as well, I am sorry." I have never managed to truly believe in your benevolence and my anarcho-atheism has always dwelled deep at the bottom of my ever skeptical apathetic soul. To sum this up: Buddhists have also believed in that vacuum filled with sheer nothingness, that great Void, but unlike myself who dreaded it, they rejoiced in it! The Christians, the Jews, the Muslims, Buddhists and Zoroastrians—all of them were guaranteed some afterlife, in Paradise or elsewhere, only I was bathing in my atheist heritage in this very feverish life which was coming to its end.

Darshan, or the slow procession moving toward Krisna's stupa and ending there, has lasted long indeed. The believers were banging at the wooden timpani while singing O HARA HARA and also stopping every ten seconds to light oil lamps. Once you entered the procession you could not leave it easily, except if you were riding a horse. So you stand, waiting your turn, you pivot, scratch your nose or hands—the same feeling as when you entered some administrative office in the West and there, in a long line, you have to wait your turn.

Belesh must have put a lot of time trying to locate me in that endless crowd, and once he spotted me he sort of dragged me out, put me into his rickshaw and this time drove fast back to Keralayeem. In our center, all the members of our group were more than surprised to hear my stories about the ocean tsunami, the disappearance of my glasses and Krisna's temple far, far away in another state of India. In fact they were all ecstatic. I returned, safe and sound, in other words, and still alive. They remembered they left me just a couple of hours ago in the bungalow, surrounded by a number of medications against a heavy case of malaria, tucked into bed. Renan de Germain, our teacher, had even offered his own private, comfortable room to me that morning—he was staying in a luxurious hotel in Cochin and wanted to transfer me there.

A long journey to Paris ahead of us, and just the idea of getting on a plane in a day or so seemed such an incredible task. But the idea of staying in a hotel made me sick! No, all I needed was a piece of turquoise sky, a piece of music, a piece of an old temple or a piece of ocean and I would feel better—I should not be ungrateful, I should give everyone credit when credit's due.

I needed all these pills I got from this group composed of crazy French yogis as they also helped me feel much better. Renan was visibly disappointed by my refusal—he wondered if I'd thought he would put me into one of those hotels, like the *Kashi Lab Mukti Bavana* in Varanasi where they accept people only when they are surely about to die, most likely a week after they checked in.

We are talking here about the oldest and the most populated Indian city, Varanasi, situated in the state of Utar Pradesh, on the west bank of the Ganges. It is also the religious center of India, the center of Hinduism where millions traditionally visit when they feel they are about to die. They come to this city so their ashes can be scattered over the Ganges, as it Is a big, huge chance for them to interrupt their personal *samsara* cycle. In this way they would stop being reborn again and thus obtain *moksha*, or final liberation.

In Varanasi the funeral companies represent the biggest industry, as many people come to die and then their bodies burn for seven days, non-stop. At the Manikarnika Ghat, in the funeral parlors, a couple of hundred bodies are placed on burning stretchers every day. First they place the corpses on stretchers, then embalm them with *Ghi,* which is a sort of transparent buttery product. The corpses have been properly washed in the Ganges and dressed up as if they were being sent to a glamorous party uptown. They burn them in the open, in pits specially made for this collective cremation.

I had to persuade Renan that such a possibility had never crossed my mind; no, I know he would not conceive of such a destiny for me, although we all know out of experience that each individual destiny could take an unexpected turn when least expected. My best friend, Ira Cohen, had his best friend burnt here, Angus McLease, who was a founding member of the Velvet Underground. But Angus, as a Tibetan Buddhist, was burnt in a funeral pyre according to the Tibetan rites. Ira told me that it was impossible to ask the local authorities to grant him a funeral in the so-called Western tradition. But I am sure Angus would not have been bothered to decide on his burial, even if they had asked him to do so. Ira carried his urn through India for a long time, all the way to his hometown in Massachusetts. However, none of this was likely to be my fate! Even though the very thought of their friendship, the idea that such friendship could have existed, made me feel great! So I felt much better, I did not want to die there and that was that!

THE LAST EVENING IN KERALAYEEM and COCHIN

It was our last evening in Keralayeem. The following morning we set out to Cochin on a small boat. We left our lagoons filled with mosquitoes and malaria, those noble coconut palms and banana trees, but, alas, like Herzog's *Nosferatu*, the malaria traveled with us on the boat. The waves of heated fever came upon me then parted in snatches, although I tried not to give in, and not allow it to entirely settle into my fit, invaded body. We walked through Cochin the whole day. There were huge Chinese fishing nets that could collect more than a few tons of fish at once. Vasco da Gama brought them over from China in the 16th century.

We took a walk through the port and arrived at the first Christian church ever erected in India, built by Da Gama as soon as he landed here. Also, his tomb, a grave for a really tiny, short man. He was such a small guy, but at the same time big—his one meter and forty centimeter height was engraved into human history. On a portrait from that century his noble, aristocratic face shines. However—I know how he died! In that church we have just mentioned there are wooden poles mounted along the aisles. The climate is so humid and heavy here in Cochin that heavy brocade curtains in the shape of a fan were stitched to these poles so the slaves could cool the air during the Christian mass. The slaves had to work them up and down.

Next to the famous music institute named after Ali Akbar Khan, there is a square gives way to the oldest Jewish quarter. We visited the old Temple, the synagogue was open, in this city where only four Jewish families remained, more precisely seven people—the rest having moved to Israel, the guide informed us.

Some of my wealthier companions insisted on visiting the palace of the rajah of Cochin, but the guide opted for a modest version of it, a Mogul palace turned into a shop of rare furniture and antiques. The objects in it modeled after the pieces of furniture that once adorned the Taj Mahal. These imitations were entirely available and on sale today in this shop. It's there I spotted the most beautiful object my eyes ever set on: it was a small table with golden, turquoise and cobalt-blue incrustations in enamel—but it really resembled some object made out of foam, slid in here from that distant, 1001-and-one-nights illuminated drawing. It reminded really of one of the walls of the Alhambra palace in Seville. I sank into the surface of that table, I fell into a deep psychedelic slumber and there was no return from it.

I sank deep into that arabesque meditation, heard the shop owner's voice, as from a distance, encouraging me to purchase the table.

"Ah, there's no use to negotiate," I said trying to defend myself from his frontal salesman's attack. "My bank card is blocked and we are staying here only tonight, just passing through this town." But he persisted—pounced on me like a hawk, using all known and unknown selling techniques. Not a single merchant from the *Nights* could had been more persuasive.

"Take it—you will pay for it when you get back home, today it is not a complicated thing to do. You can send money through any bank or through Western Union. I can tell you are a very nice lady I trust you I know you are not going to cheat me. In fact madam, YOU should visit our region in India... ," he slowly and slyly advanced with his gig. He ordered his assistant to bring me a chair, a coffee and two lokums as he continued: "Our region is like a pearl, an emerald in comparison to this humid hole named Kerala..." He was adding oil to his fiery speech, "and just to tell you, we have MANY beautiful objects, even nicer than your table.."

YOUR TABLE!

These words banged my head like a hammer, sounded like some magic formula after which the owner and his brother, both originally from Kashmir, persuaded me to sink into a huge armchair. I felt weak and feverish and they were bringing lots of teas and sweets. After a while they sold me the table. They brought in a piece of scratched paper which they made me sign and I could not really see, neither the table's price nor the other text I was about to sign. They said they would deliver it, send it on a boat 40 days after they got the money, but as I continued to shake my head incredulously, they sat down and both, in one voice, told me the following story—We all knew the world we were living in was completely taken over by Shaytan, Iblis, but in such a dishonest world, these guys were the law-abiding citizens under Shariya law. They did not cheat their clients, they reassured. I decided I was going to trust them—that table was a colorful gem made in carved wood and considering it was a real arabesque coming from a craftsman's workshop it was not really expensive by Western standards.

The evening was coming to its end. I went with two lady accountants to a Portuguese restaurant. These two really made me change my mind about accountants as they were very open minded and eager to learn something. At the restaurant's table there was our teacher, Renan, surrounded by the rest of our group. I believed I had an opportunity to really shut everyone's mouth this time. Perhaps I should have done earlier, but it was useful, these people had to be told something! When one of these racists sitting here (I cannot recall if that was Racist number 2 or Racist number 3) greeted me with "Mina!"—and that was the fiftieth consecutive time on that very trip alone, I went off my rocker:

"Oh, shame on you so-called yoga practitioners! You say you are trained in concentration and utmost focusing—how come you still cannot learn my name which is rather short and you have already pronounced it here at least 50 times!" But this was not the end; in fact as dinner advanced, it went going from bad to worse.

After dinner, which consisted entirely of two glasses of water mixed with the powder of quinine and aspirin, I refused to pay an exorbitant price, ridiculously high for any world restaurant, let alone India.

Everyone knows my generosity toward the Other as a part of my Dharma training has been proverbial and "Nina has always had the role of Santa Claus, in all regular friendly and family gatherings, since kindergarten." Perhaps I would treat all of these people as I do my friends and colleagues at any other restaurant, but I opened my purse and realized I had forgotten my wallet at the hotel. So when the waiter was waiting on us, I asked one of the racists to lend me money in order for me to go back to the hotel and fetch my purse, but she exclaimed in a resigned and affected voice "ach, you see, Tina or Mina refuses to pay her part!"

That was a mean unsolicited remark and I snapped: "Shame on you! How could you lie so much in front of everyone? I have never said I refuse to pay my bill and hey! Look at you—how dare you talk to me this way? No respect here for the big Other, according to Levinas or whoever may be listening?"

They remained silent, and in fact as heavy silence reigned for some good ten good minutes, Renan took out his purse and paid for the entire dinner. He then left with three other friends "on a night about town," while the rest of us boarded a minibus that took us straight to the airport's hotel. Our saga came to an end. I did not say good-bye to any of the members of this highly eccentric group. I took an elevator to the fifth floor of this faceless, postmodern hotel, nested in the very heart of the airport. My flight was scheduled the following day, eleven in the morning. Weather was sunny and nice, not heavy, and that was good as this time we were to change planes not in Riyadh but in the Saudi-Arabian city of Jeddah. It seemed it was perfect timing to leave late in the morning—the hotel room was well air-conditioned which created a certain fantasy-promise that I was almost sure I would get a good night's sleep.

I sort of underestimated the predictions my natal chart and horoscope have always warned about: I was never going to relax in any human situation simply because my life was filled with unpredictable, last-minute turns and adventures. Because something happened that very night just as I was getting ready to put pajamas on and to sleep, something very bad—and that was an attack of the biggest and most exhausting fever I ever had in my life. I was turning helplessly one side of bed to the other; and I would get overwhelmed by a very hot fever which dried and burned my mouth every couple of minutes. This attack was quickly followed by another—I would get cold and shiver, as if I were lying in the midst of the North Pole, completely naked in the coldest snow! I was shaking with the hotel bed. I could even hear the mattress producing a funny sound as I was moving left to right. Oh that's a bad sign, I thought to myself—this commotion really recalled the days of terrible malaria in West Africa more than forty years ago. And what was more than evident now was the fact I could not dream of leaving this bed and hotel room the next day, whether I decided to travel on, or not. That is, if I were still, as a person, in my right mind.

Guess what happened? Early that morning, I somehow managed to tame my legs and at a certain point I came out of it. As I was entirely in some altered state of feverish mind, call it a temporary coma or whatever it might be, I packed my cosmetics and suitcase and made my way to the airport, not really knowing or remembering how I did so. I cannot even strain my poor brain into remembering the way I climbed on board, and the descriptive facts concerning my eight-hour flight to Jeddah.

Jeddah was the place we were to change flights and so I boarded a plane to Paris. But I do remember distinctly regarded my peripatetic walk up and down airport corridors in Cochin. This walk got condensed into some sort of deistic image I already had in mind and never to leave. I turned around for hours looking for the local pharmacy. Everyone at the airport directing me "somewhere over there," reassuring me such a place really existed, and when I finally found it I realized I had not only left the customs security area but that I'd compulsively bought a heap of useless, unnecessary medications. There was a homeopathic remedy, the thing that one swallows after first signs of malaria, but I had largely passed over that stage… and there were some Indian aspirins, probably forbidden by the world health organization. Anyhow, they were hard to swallow and as I tried nonetheless they glued to my gall bladder—I could not breathe any longer.

JEDDAH, JANUARY 7, 2015

Despite everyone and in spite of everything promised and even things not promised to us, I found the Saudis very simple and warm people. After I put the obligatory thin veil over my face and after I wished everyone a pleasant "Salaam Aleykoum," I approached the stand for the passengers in transit where they gave me numerous vouchers for various meals at their airport, but, alas, I was not able to swallow food any longer. I complained to a junior pilot by the stand, that I felt a very strange weakness in my body. He took pity on me and directed me towards a special lounge on the building's second floor. He signed a special voucher for me which I promptly took to the VIP lounge, the waiting room for Important and extremely Rich Saudis. I slept there in a convertible chair for a good ten hours, surrounded by other happy travelers in transit and finders of this tiny Eden. Then they announced my flight to Paris, but just before I was about to board the plane, I caught myself thinking about these people whose rigidity was somehow combined with the utmost tenderness, a strange sentiment which really moved me. Two air-hostesses came to fetch and take me to the plane, and they were almost dying of laughter as they recounted to me things I did or said—but I had no recollection of any of it. As I was hallucinating more than dreaming in the lounge, the surveying doctor at the airport came to see me. According to these ladies, he really insisted on keeping me in one of Jeddah's hospitals. Eventually he decided to leave me there in their lounge. He prescribed big shots of quinine and vitamins every few hours and a total surveillance of my case, whatsoever happenened. They could not predict the outcome of my journey.

If I were to wake and open my eyes before they announced the flight, which I indeed managed, they would place me onto the plane while explaining at the same time what was to be done later, where I'd go, what to do in case of an emergency before I reached my final destination—the Institute of Tropical Diseases in Paris.

I survived that trip rather cheerfully due to their intense care and attention. By the time we reached Charles de Gaulle, I had almost forgotten I had been ill—however, the insane situation at that airport made me feel worse than ever: the passengers from Asia to Paris were to face a very difficult landing. The massacre of the *Charlie Hebdo* editorial board had happened the day before we arrived, so all security officers were both cursing and accusing Saudis of being the most dreadful terrorists on Earth. As for me—these people stay until this day in the most pleasant memory as the warmest, most charming part of the Arab universe.

EGYPT

I often travelled to Africa and I even lived there twice, but out of that enormous continent I loved the best the queen of all these ancient cradles of civilizations, the country called Egypt. I was given the opportunity to visit several times: my first trip to Egypt comes to my memory in snatches, but was the best and the most romantic one. The last one—just before the explosion of Arab Spring, was both the most difficult and the heaviest. Socially speaking it was the most unacceptable. Before the Muslim Brothers came to power they began announcing their religious program through the endless singing of the *muezzins* in the *minarets* of the improvised mosques scattered along banks of the Nile. They spread in the distance every fifty meters along the road from Cairo to Aswan. Amenhotep and Amon Ra seemed to have disappeared for good, and endless Surah which the priests read through the speakers in the minarets, were there to remind us of dreadful repetitive operas of the Western postmodern political concept, and those of composers such as Philip Glass. I will not talk much about that last trip.

My first trip was terribly romantic. I stepped onto the soil of "my Africa" which I had to leave twenty years earlier under dramatic circumstances due to illness, malaria, a young woman that I was once upon that time. I used to laugh at authors who somewhat like Karen Blixen, tried to describe the continent. What could have been said on the side of the colonizers about a continent which was the cradle of us all trying to swing us gently into all directions? This time I was sent by my local paper to follow, largely from the distance, the escalation of the first war in Iraq. Everything seemed to be peaceful and "quiet" in Egypt, aside from the obligatory soldiers posted at some outposts, to make sure there wouldn't be any upsurge or rebellion, along the road which stretched from Cairo towards the Red Sea and Mount Sinai. In Egypt itself there were no war incidents so I could devote my discreet activities to the exploration of "ancient civilization"—waiting for me nearby.

KAIRO-LUXOR-ASWAN, 1990

By the end of August I found myself in Cairo, and then I went further south to the Egyptian summer resorts and to well-known local archeological sites, mirages of the ancient civilization, Aswan and Luxor. If you ask an Arab about the issues of the Iraqi-Egyptian conflict he will wave his hand with a somewhat casual dismissal: the entire history and culture of this country is permeated with the mystical belief that life is just a part of a larger destiny, an old Maghreb philosophy. As a consequence of such assumptions I will supply the following story.

Upon our arrival in Luxor, the old capitol of Thebes on the eastern bank of the Nile, it became obvious to us all the temples in it were steadily being destroyed by Christian and Moslem raids and attacks, I would say twice as much as those temples we visited travelling up the river.

The oldest temple in Luxor, originally built by Amenophis III and situated on a very ancient sanctuary was the temple devoted to Amon, then to goddess Nutt as well as to her son Horus, lord of the Moon.

Amenhotep, the anarchist ruler had transferred the greater part of the temple to his new capital, Tel Amarna, but the temple was completely restored during the consequent rule of the great Egyptian warrior, Ramses II. This tallest man of ancient Egypt (he was 1.8m) adorned the temple with his own representations—the statues and the reliefs where he was conquering disobedient Hittites and all the rest who could read the relief and use it as a practical warning against rebellion. At the very entrance to the temple a long colonnade of sphinxes, as well as in the temples of Karnak which used to be connected by these colonnades to Luxor (the road between them was 2.5 kilometers).

At the entrance to this temple there were two obelisks erected (one 24 meters tall the other 26) which today belong to the French. They managed to take one of them to Paris, during Napoleon's conquests, but the other was too heavy so they left it. However, many people were eager to obtain that poor temple throughout the ages: Ramses had knocked down statues of Amenophis III, and today there is a big court of Ramses II erected, adorned with alabaster statues of the young king Tutankhamun. There were also low reliefs representing scenes from the gathering of people during festivities of "OPET", processions from Luxor to Karnak.

From this courtyard we enter the yard of Amenophis II (or Amenhotep II), with the double columns which oddly enough still kept the vivid colors once painted with. The very yard opens to a ***hypostyle*** turned later by the end of the 4th century A.D. into emperor Justinian's church. Reliefs there were covered by plaster and a new imagery emerged, the lives of saints, painted over the reliefs. Funny thing though is these frescoes were heavily ruined and washed out through time and the original Amenophis III's reliefs emerge now intact in their beauty.

The history of Egypt is the story of layers and as I wish to return to some original traces of its story, I will put the tourist guide aside having decided to bear witness to its story all by myself. I walked through Luxor quickly and casually in the morning to come back to its site alone that very evening and without any tourists.

When I arrived to Amon Ra's temple in Karnak strange winds started blowing; it grew dark very quickly. I was eager to find the temples so that I would not lose my directions in the dark. These were the temples of god Ptah and his wife, the ferocious lioness Sekhmet, as well as the temples of the god of war, Montu, the goddess Nut and the god Khensu. I remained in the dilapidated temple of Ramses III a bit longer than in other temples, though not longer than half an hour, but the reason it took me a bit longer was due to my feeling that the temple had, in fact, nothing to do with the temple we had visited that very morning. The atmosphere in it was mysterious and foreboding. The wind howling ominously through the abandoned walls of the temple raising with it the dusty red sand coming from the desert.

I looked towards the North throwing a glance at the ancient ruins of Amon Temple. All I could observe were low bushes sprinkled with sand dunes and sporadic traces of donkey's hooves. I remember an Arab had recommended this road to me that morning, and he said I should find the temple of god Ptah, located just next to the temple of Montu. I knew Ptah was the god of writers, artists and artisans as well; allegedly he was the creator of the world, a magician, the Egyptian Hermes. I did not know even this much about his comrade Montu, except that he was a fearsome god of War. In the British guidebook it was written "the temple of Ptah was surely worth visiting, however, it seemed a very difficult task to achieve". It had a reputation of being difficult to access. I looked at my watch. It was exactly 4:30pm.

The last rays of dying sun were penetrating the huge pylons of Amon's temple. It would seem simply ridiculous that I came all the way to this spot and failed to find the temple of my favorite deity, the writers' god Ptah. I was turning around eager to see one of the local Arab guides who otherwise used to be more than eager to help any tourist for a symbolic *baksheesh* in return. There was no trace of them, probably all gone home by now. While I turned to overlook the highest dune with a huge abandoned patch of earth behind it, I spotted the foot of a nearby hill with a tiny group of people all in deep blue *djellabas*—they were waving, calling me to come and join them. I saw myself jumping over dunes and when I reached them I uttered in a low voice "Montu"? "Ptah?" One of these men asked me in return who I was and where I was coming from, and visibly assuaged that I came from Yugoslavia he exclaimed:

"Nasser! Tito! Great friends!" He took me by the hand and led me to a well guarded temple, whose keeper I assume he was in person.

He opened a vestibule then took me to a courtyard framed by sixteen pillars. Behind this yard a stretch of three chapels—one darker from the other, all of them firmly locked. I stopped for a second. At that very moment I forgot everything I read in the guidebook and decided to trust my preservation instinct which was telling me not to advance. However, my Arab companion insisted on continuing: "Cmon, you have to see something." A strange glow lit his eyes or perhaps this was a part of my hallucination.

He took me to the first chapel, needless to mention he had the keys to it, and in that hidden space the headless statue of Ptah, seated at the gate, welcomed us. Oh there was the statue of Amon, the central deity of ancient Egypt, but he was a bit hidden behind his comrade Ptah. The Arab dragged me to the chamber which was kept locked, located on the right. He unlocked that door—not a single streak of light in there! I directed my gaze upwards—in the middle of the ceiling a hole allowing light to penetrate the room but at that hour this was fairly impossible. A very heavy smell of incense and burning candles reigned over the room and in its middle—a huge statue of the angry goddess Sekhmet. This goddess was but an angry aspect of the peaceful and lovable deity Bastet. Where Bastet stood for peace and love, Sekhmet stood for famine, wars and diseases. Her unique place of cult and worship in the world remained in the temple of Ptah in Egypt, this particular one where I was standing half-paralyzed with fear, suffocating from the smell of heavy incense. My knees were enfeebled, giving way so I couldn't move. I heard the Arab yelling at me "touch her heart, touch it—it will bring you luck!"

Oh I gave it a thought with the entire naiveté of my early thirties. I had nothing to lose I thought as I touched her frozen heart, hidden under the cover of heavy marble and black basalt.

I wanted to leave the chapel right away. It took me a second to understand that the cult of the goddess was still alive and it existed in some form other than the ancient. It was probably hidden from our Western gaze but I was able to recognize it once I found myself there.

It did cross my mind perhaps Sekhmet would avenge me for entering her temple uninvited and not initiated to her cult. What if I hurt and desacralized the space which I suddenly fell into? I remembered all the legends about the cursed pharaohs—in a way, I had already possessed the presentiment that one was not supposed to enter these spaces. So where did I get such a strong and parallel impulse urging me to visit the complex of Karnak that evening? Who prompted me to look for the closed temples in order to photograph them one more time?

All these questions crossed my mind as I was

slowly walking backwards to exit the chapel and then, I tripped on an object and fell. My glasses flew down and simultaneously with the Arab guide, I fell on my knees to collect them. I noticed his face had duly turned into an evil mask as we found ourselves on the floor, or perhaps it only seemed so. My glasses fell next to the Goddess's pedestal and the double darkness fell on me as well. Finally we found them in that space and soon enough regained our way.

I gave the Arab double *baksheesh* for taking me out, and then he suggested, much to my relief, to take me to Montu's temple. Montu's temple was under restoration but in front of it the resplendent statue of Montu, the Egyptian god of war, reigned.

It was 1990s, Montu's status was quickly "restored" not in Egypt but in my home country which we called Yugoslavia.

I left this particular temple quickly, only to return to the temple of Amon Ra. I noticed less than some thirty minutes expired from the time I decided to head north from the first sandy dune I had spotted on my way. At this particular moment—and we are all likely to agree here- every normal person on Earth would have decided to leave this area quickly; alas, not me.

As if I had been taken by some indescribable force, I was urged to explore the labyrinth of Amon's temple which its last visitors had deserted quite a while ago. In order to gain some courage I switched my tiny Walkman on and soon enough completely calmed listening to the divine voice of Maria Callas. At a certain moment I turned back and observed a young man who had rhythm and visiting speed similar to mine, and who somewhat like me, was himself still visiting the temples. It felt good to know I was not the only tourist. I approached and asked if he had known where the Sacred Lake was. That place I observed earlier in the morning and had it seemed interesting. He pointed his hand and resembling a bit the White Rabbit from *Alice in Wonderland*, he answered shortly: "Behind that wall."

I started walking in that direction but he did not follow me.

I continued in that direction and got completely lost. I never made it to the Sacred (Scarab's) Lake, but soon I found myself surrounded by the ugly headless statues of Ramses II, as well as some huge stones inscribed with reliefs hard to read. The only visible scripture on the reliefs were the heads of cobras and deadly scarabs. I returned to the huge yard which was meant to hold ceremonies of Tuthmosis III where I had left the charming young man who tried to show me the directions. I discovered at its entrance a huge Nubian who offered me his services as guide by suggesting he walk me to the lake. I told him I had no *baksheesh* left, to which he casually waved his hand and said he didn't mind guiding me for free—he would take me to a special place where I'd be able to snap a unique photo of the most exquisite alabaster statue of the late queen Hatshepsut and her royal entourage.

We followed winding stairs to a premonitory of the temple almost entirely in ruins and which stood as a solitary group of ruins on the west side of the Sacred Lake. As it was getting late, I realized I would not be able to take photos. In order not to sadden my kind host I kept on clicking even knowing my film was already used. The Nubian, who was very agile, climbed the rocks as quickly as a big cat, then he took me by the hand and suddenly exclaimed: "Come over here, I'll show you something *extraordinary*!"

Time stood still and I obeyed, as if under a spell; I followed him while my heart emitted beats made of stone.

I was sure my own heart was so pure nothing ugly could ever happen to it. We arrived at the place the official guidebook called "the eastern gate" and where one was "unable to climb the ruins."

We managed to climb that monument. The Nubian was helping me, crisscrossing his hands so I would stand on them, pushing me upward and there, all of a sudden once we finished climbing—a tiny chapel stood with a beautiful statue of Tutankhamun. The gentle and childlike face of the early disappeared pharaoh was carved in yellow alabaster and completely saved from the ravages of time. My guide approached the statue and lay my hand on his head; then took my hand and placed it on the statue's shoulder, gently, while at the same time whispering prayers and kissing the statue.

His action appeared quite crazy to me and I began wondering how I was to escape this sudden and newly created situation. He turned to me with a serious expression and asked me to recite a one-minute prayer to the pharaoh which I obeyed, a hand rested on the pharaoh's marble shoulder, as if I also held the invisible symbol of *ankh*.

Afterwards we descended the wall slowly. As we were descending he showed me the relief of that great protector of all temples queen Hatshepsut, who was obviously, as I came to learn, his very own house deity.

We walked along the narrow path exiting the ruins and he was singing "Hatshepsut! Hatshepsut!" He told me then he lived exclusively among the temples' ruins at Karnak and his daily sustenance came solely from the *baksheesh* given to him by random tourists.

At the exit of this complex I shrugged my shoulders and told him I hadn't had anything on me, not even ten *piasters* to give.

I have nothing! I repeated, showing him at that point the tip of my left small finger, indicating there was no money in my bag to which he waved his hand and smiled one of his good-natured smiles.

I also noticed at that point complete darkness had enveloped Karnak at that very hour I realized we had become friends.

****

Twenty years later as I was lying bed-ridden, tied to my pillows by some "heavy and chronic disease," my son who was then a young pupil but today distinguished doctor of virology, came by with the idea of how to save his mother's life by applying a very radical method. "Mother, if you survive all this," the youngster hardly swallowed up his own words, "you have to promise that we will visit Egypt together and you will return to the temple of Sekhmet. You'll have to apologize to her for entering her sanctuary disrespectfully."

That's how it happened—my last visit to Luxor included an offering of flowers and fruits to this evil goddess whose somber altar was attended by that time by the Muslim Brothers. From that moment, it seemed the Goddess left my household peaceful, as she seemed to be too busy elsewhere, spreading her evil actions throughout Egypt as much as everywhere else in the world.

ITALY

PART 1 (Roma)

Airport Charles de Gaulle (Paris)
—Leonardo da Vinci (Roma)
February-March 2008

February 29, 2008

Vladi and I enter a huge lobby at Charles de Gaulle Airport and the kid tells me confidentially: "Mom, please do not stay longer neither in the loo nor in the Duty Free. You know I always get scared when you say you're leaving for a minute and then I do not see you for three hours… ok, just kidding, but the plane will take off without us if you get stuck in there, shopping."

On an Alitalia plane all the girls (and here I mean hostesses) resemble Lydia and Emma. "You see, my son," I tell him, "your grandmother and your aunt are REAL Italians, they all resemble one another, these girls come from the north of Italy—they have hair color of ash and soft dark eyes." My son also has something of that soft sweet character, the same as, say, Michelangelo's sense of soft curve and beauty; the same soft tender eyes with a sweet look—he is a real Mediterranean, as much as my own mother was and her Istrian, Italian family. Oddly enough, his paternal grandmother looks just the same. An incredible coincidence made these two ladies look alike. At any rate, this trip is our real return to the "family roots".

March 1 2008

We are in the very center of Rome! And here is the colossal Colosseum, without the statue of Nero, but there are numerous tourists instead. It's a cold day in March. Antonia, our hostess, is lovely in her hospitality and Lualda does her best to reciprocate our hospitality which she enjoyed at our house in Paris. We take a walk through the Colosseum and I am at lengths to explain to Vladi its interior, I believe I'm doing it better than any Italian *cicerone*. See, these are the cages where they kept gladiators and in these cells here they kept wild beasts. I try to imitate my own father who was an encyclopedia, but that one is truly hard to copy: he knew almost everything about ancient Rome and all ancient civilizations whereas I know nothing about them.

Lualda comes to our rescue going further into the details of the history of the Romans, with her also inimitable voice of a professional art historian, greatly unimpressed and completely indifferent to the beauty of the local landscape. She tries to classify the facts chronologically. She takes us down the road of Forum Romanum up to Capitol Hill. This particular road has been trampled under the walking feet of numerous tourists so it was being restored.

"Everything is under the reconstruction!" she exclaims. "And they are still trying to find emperor Nero's golden house, but they are never going to find the site. It disappeared, swallowed entirely by the Middle Ages, the way the more recent epoch buried vestiges of the Middle Ages—look at our silly Vittorio Emmanuele's done to the valuable monuments—he erased them to build a road to his stupid monument, oh yes, he destroyed the original citadel of Rome! Rome was originally extended from north to south, and this idiot insisted on enlarging the town from east to west, so he situated the city upside down so that his urban invention has blocked the traffic completely ever since. It is more that painful to move through the city in any given way but by foot."

Lualda knows the city quite well. She participated in restoration of almost every historic site and monument, thus the first thing she asked us was "which Rome would you like to see" Baroque Rome, Renaissance Rome, antique Rome, early Christian Rome or the modern one? For each of them, she gasped, an innocent visitor would need a couple of months to see or even a couple of years, depending on his personal timing and effort. And without waiting for an answer she takes us to the Basilics and further down to Capitolino insisting Vladimir drinks water from a special fountain, "so he will have only male children".

"This is the place where Romans get married. I got married here too", she explains in a proud voice. She takes us to a café where we drink lemonade and eat a big chocolate cake; she rejoices at mothering both of us—me and my son. All our disputes melt away and evaporate into fine mist of that cold Roman afternoon.

I don't mention anything to her but she reads in my expression a certain loneliness, hurt and abandonment.

Eventually I tell her: "You know, something terrible has happened—they tried to take my child away." Simultaneously, I remember my father and our first trip to Italy. Now I have understood how he must have felt during that trip. He appeared sad and at the same time rather joyful, hard to explain—in fact, he appeared as a man threatened by the loss, his child but who managed to postpone a certain legal jurisdiction. Funny that he never expressed his emotions, at least never verbalised them in this way. However, I know his gaze was somewhat detached and melancholic, like De Chirico's paintings, and the only thing he ever said during that trip was "You know, your dad has loved you a lot, he cares a lot for you, perhaps even too much for your own good."

It seems I've never thought about his presence in my life during the whole time he was with us. But now as he was absent, and his absence stretched over a good period of three years, I realised that even the mourning period was somewhat taken away from me. I have never gotten enough time to digest his death. It was like the time for any reflection was gone. I've had no time to reflect upon my parents' recent departure, nor any time to myself in order to read and write, the activities which were supposed to mark my entire being.

As I was walking with Lualda and Vladi towards

piazza Venezia (the only Venetian building in the entire city), my memories were coming back as well as the notion of "my" time and pace in this space—everything was coming back to me.

We arrived at a building where "il Duche" Mussolini gave his first speech from a certain balcony. That spot bore no mark or an official plate commemorating the event so it seemed to me, all of a sudden, the city of Rome, just like me, has been trying to remember its real history which was often neglected by historians.

It seemed we stumbled upon Antonia's house quite by chance, in a romantic quarter "san Giovanni di Laterano," and we were happy to be back. We grew hungry from that long walk so made dinner, turned the TV on and watched the Hollywood blockbuster "Gladiator."

March 2, 2008

I got up early eager to run all over this big city with my little boy, but as I tripped on my pyjamas in the bathroom, I took it as a sign I should slow so I sat down and started reading. Correspondence and memories of Jacques-Alain Muller, Lacan's son-in-law. I dragged myself in my pyjamas the whole morning until early afternoon.

I start became jealous of my reading hours as people start appropriating them, devouring them by their own motives till I'm almost on my knees—I'm willing to trade anything, almost everything for my own free hours.

In fact, take it back—I would not trade hours spent with my son or some old, reliable friends—the time I spend with them is precious. If the friends are of long standing, they are precious; however, if a shade of doubt crosses our friendship then time with them turns uncomfortable, almost an irritable experience.

Lualda calls us at 2pm sharp, she is impatient and insists on meeting us right away in front of the Colosseum. As she had originally invited us here and as her invitation was generous and beautiful, it is hard for me to turn down any of her moody suggestions. And that's the real characteristic of this social trap. Lualda was not the brightest and the most loving of all my girlfriends, or at least that's how I thought of her for quite a while, but she showed a rare sensitivity inviting us to Italy. She invited us to this magnificent and dilapidated Roman *palazzo* to stay with her for a couple of weeks while her friend Antonia is away. We managed to find inexpensive plane tickets to go to Rome, but we haven't managed to cater to some better social atmosphere which would make Lualda feel more relaxed.

We rushed to meet her in front of the Colosseum but when we got there she had already felt tired, she said, as well as obliged to take us down the steep road all the way to the Roman Forum. Yes, and there the temple of the Vestals, she stormed, and here they spilled onto the *plebs* Caesar's ashes, the monument to Vittorio Emanuele a horrible work of art, Campo Marcio a respectable site where she participated in local excavations a long time ago.

Bernini was still resplendent in *piazza Navona*, fountain *Di Trevi* was still the most beautiful fountain in the world, and Carravagio left his best work in the church St Louis de Francesi. However, her mood had considerably darkened when we reached *piazza Farnesi* where her late husband, Maurizio, worked for a while. She entered into a spiral of telling about that difficult period when many friends abandoned her. Marco was a creep, and his wife Helen just a plain idiot.

We are in search for the perfect ice-cream but not a single ice-cream parlour is good enough to house us. At that very moment Vladi remembers he did not close the doors of our terrace correctly, and at hearing this, Lualda has almost lost her mind. All of a sudden we have to take a taxi back to the apartment, the ride was overpriced but I have to pay. We discover in the apartment things to be in the perfect order, but Lualda kept her rage. There was not a single ghost of a chance for any reflexion on her side for mood-recovery, she could not bear a thought of any pardon.

She was born in the horror and restraint of our Gulag, named *Goli Otok*, so she hasn't been given a chance to forget. She continued complaining, gossiping friends and relatives while downing a bottle of Chianti, then, all of a sudden and as if propelled by some dark force, she jumps up and says "OK, now I should go and I will not be able to meet with you before your departure!"

I know some people try to put their life on the right track and turn to good direction, but then stop and tire easily. Some of them do not even try to change for the better; some drink a lot and she is one although her doctor told her even a drop of alcohol would be detrimental to her health.

I admire her ability to move through all these situations, now that she has already lost direction in life and the command of her inner GPS—it was such a sad life resembling uncontrollable clamour. I was shocked to see her at the edge of survival, and yes, of course, she was entitled to any folly—but I was not that hero or rather heroine who could wipe mud from her face or who would lift burden off her crooked back…

March 4, 2008

I woke early again and spent a considerable sum of money which happens often as the result of getting up early. I figured to treat myself to something, as if I needed a treat to assuage my trauma at getting up so early.

I spent 30 euros in a supermarket, now I'm making these sandwiches; another 8 euros for the subway train tickets, tickets to enter the Vatican—22 euros, oh, also 3 euros for rosary beads. I gave them to Vlad to scrutinise, and this necklace I bought for his grandmother Lydia. He was exceptionally calm the whole visit to the Vatican. I took to making an exorbitant number of photos. I photographed *The Last Judgment* in Saint Peter's church from all possible angles as well as *The Pieta.*

"Mother," he asks all of a sudden, "Is this the Church of Churches? I have never seen anything THIS beautiful!" he rejoiced. It is beautiful, he likes beauty and I know he deserves all that money I don't have, but I always find something for him regardless. He is sweet and good-natured, the way his father used to be, but my ex lost that quality throughout the years which crumbled all the closeness we have had. At any rate, after all the trouble I've had with my health this is one peaceful and healing journey, soon to be completed in my new book entitled *The Cure.*

We return to Antonia's place and meet with Anne, a teacher in the French *lycée Michel Montaigne* but on holiday in Rome. She brought my telephone book which I forgot in Paris and the numbers of Enzo Cucchi and Carla Baruchello. Cucchi's number I still knew by heart and believed that I would never forget it but these last two years of chemo had erased several layers from my memory.

This very afternoon I was climbing piazza d'Espagna with my son, and then slowly through park Borghese, telling him the story of my unusual encounter with the painter. I took him to café Rosatti and to Piazza di Popolo so that he could taste the best ice-cream in the world. Enzo took me there to try the same product, traces of a vanilla in an otherwise strawberry ice-cream. After our painful experience with Lualda last night the boy hated even the thought of an ice-cream.

"Let's not go, mom! Not really, that place seems expensive and I know we don't have money for sweets."

It is not easy to be a poor parent, the kids feel all that. Just that very morning in the church of the Vatican he spelled the dictum written on a curtain "Let the Almighty guide you through all dark forests." The good wishes and desires of a similar origin are the only things I can give him.

March 6, 2008 seventh day in Rome

I would be surprised to hear any other definition of the city of Rome but "a baroque city!" In fact, even the antique, ancient past of Rome is pre-baroque, a sort of precursor to the Baroque. Neither in ancient, classic Roman art nor in the baroque are we able to find calm Greek lines leading to harmony. I've only thought about it this morning as we observed Michelangelo's *Last Judgement*, his fury and anger, *Sturm und drang*, people pointing fingers and knives at one another, all that passion… They would place their foot on a huge snake, then play with that viper as if it were a toy, etc. And then we see a saint who reads his Bible in the minds of all that fury and hurricane whilst the sky cracks open around him. Well, that's a perfect portrait of me.

We walked through Celio for hours, watched that perfect park bathe in sunlight, with hundreds of green long-tailed parakeets flying through the ancient treetops (parakeets were our household deities before they flew away and we lost our house soon afterwards.) As we enjoyed that frozen, green moment of eternity I noticed that even park Celio was a Baroque venture!

A thought has crossed my mind that Rome is the craziest and the most baroque of all the cities I've known. In the Capitolino's museum Campidoglio, we noticed all the antique statues were *baroque.* The statue of a wounded warrior, later to be redone by Pierre—Etienne Monnot—is very baroque. Lysippus with his statues of young winged gods had their baroque sensibility. The statue of Leda from the 4th century BC made by a Greek Timoteus is a Baroque work of art. The statue of Venus Capitolina, 1st C. BC, is a heritage of Baroque as well as all the statues from Hadrian's Villa (centaurs and drunk fauns and sleepy satyrs originally made by Praxiteles). All fallen gladiators (above all "the Wounded Galatian") and wounded boys (Spinario), all of them precursors of Baroque but also precursors to expressionism.

Anne, Vladi and I were bound to find many more brilliant statues similar to the ones I've mentioned in the unforgettable Villa Borghese. We were able to touch, or rather bite at the sugar-cube of Bernini's marble which seemed to evade us, always flying away, following an indefinite serpentine curve, and the feeling from Bernini served as a sort of trade-mark for the entire architecture of the city. One was almost capable of touching physically this sentiment of Baroque in Rome. One could breath it in. One could almost pounce on it in order to strangle it, or simply start dancing along with it!

And Villa Borghese was nothing but a symbol (of this feeling, sentiment) and its own epiphany.

I could not doubt it any longer, just because of this particular feeling my father visited Rome quite often, and as soon as he entered the city he would visit Villa Borghese, to show me among other things all ancient antiquities, not only the marble statues but their *Pinacotheca*, that beautiful humid box full of exquisite paintings.

This journey rests under the sign of my late father, and under the sign of my memory of his great love for baroque painting especially of this particular corner of the world!

As I was walking with my son and grandson, Vladimir, these memories gained meaning and significance.

At Capitolino, I showed the boy not only the best work of Pietro da Cortona, Guido Reni, Pier Francesco Mola, Caravaggio, Correggio, Veronese, but I had a special pleasure (a very tender and sad, baroque pleasure) of telling which works among many his grandfather treasured. Vlad was mersmerized.

I remember the day when old Vladimir took me for the first time to Villa Borghese. My father stopped in front of Girolamo daTreviso's *Venere Dormiente* and took a really long time explaining the painting, Venus's

Baroque curves, the landscape in the background which was "influenced by Giorgione", the goddess's sleepy metaphysical face as well as her thin golden veil painted with extreme refinement.

Now My son has followed with the same inquisitive steady gaze, inherited from his grandfather, the movement of Girolamo's hand. And as he was sinking ever deeper in that painting all of a sudden I felt liberated, free. I knew he would be saved from all stupidity in this world. In the deepest sense of the word, Art will be his recluse, as it has always been to all sensitive and deep human beings.

I have accomplished my mission—and this journey has paid off, in every imaginable sense. All voyages, as well as epochs and the cities we visited, possess several layers of experience which goes with them. This voyage bore a mark of reminiscences of my parents. And where were they now when I longed so much to tell them I was so grateful because they allowed me to become an artist! And how much I missed them and how stupid my impossibility to tell them these words while they were still alive!

Lualda came to see us late that evening—she was spiffy and busy—a big change in her—and there on the Roman terrace she told me some new stories about my father and her parents. Obviously, they knew each other from the Comintern years. All of a sudden the atmosphere warmed up in Antonia's house. Both of us, girls, remembered the circumstances in which we left our country and the outlook of our homeland at that time. That was quite a bizarre epoch for Serbia, the early 1980s, but then, we wandered, was there any other era for it except for the moment of the permanent Baroque which constantly ruled in it..

March 9 2008, the tenth day in Rome

Vladi insisted we visit Campidoglio again. "There were two rooms left for us to see, mom!" He was so methodological and possessed academic stamina that his grandfather had had. I myself had never possessed that quality—at least not to their extent though.

I stayed in the museum in front of the statue of the Wounded Galatian for a long time. He had features of the French singer Johnny Hallyday who all of a sudden went bankrupt, but in reality I myself felt to be that warrior from the I century BC. I was alone among the Galatians, quite exhausted among them, a rope around my neck. The Romans were patricians, aristocrats, whereas Galatians were representatives of "plebs," ill-mannered slaves…

And yet—I respected them all, both Romans and Galatians after some good fifteen years spent with Galatians I learnt how to respect them democratically, whereas I belonged to yet another clan…

March 10 2008

The following day we went to EUR that strange neocolonial fascist quarter built in the style of early Italian futurism. Mussolini started building this area, hoping to host the Universal Exhibition in Rome in 1942. We were supposed to visit a long lost family of friends my mother liked and held in high esteem, Count de Burro and his wife countess Petrija.

I would not say aristocracy always gets on my nerves, on the contrary, but this visit truly targeted an experience for Vlad, meeting some of the rare living friends of his maternal grandmother. These folks were decent, noble-hearted bourgeoisie who did not stop for a second repeating that they "loved my mother immensely." Allegedly, my mother, in the capacity of doctor, stayed with madame Mileva, Petrija's mother for the entire two days while madam suffered severe pneumonia. They asserted skilfully that my mother left me in our apartment all alone, and as they also learnt I happened to have a slight fever and flu at the time, they concluded that mom was an incredible doctor, out of this world! Yes, mom was a wonderful doctor, perhaps much less a good mother. But yes, things like this exist in the world. Alright, Petrija de Burro did not frame all this the way I'm jotting it down now—but what she intended to say—and she was quite clear in communicating many of her overtones—she managed to make clear. This woman had quite a gift of inserting implied things but she would do it in such an elegant and unobtrusive manner! She was not "endowed" to spread around some heavy direct remarks which we were likely to find in the speech of various idiots. Take me for example, dear reader, I often hit my listeners with a heavy artillery of truths!

Then she continued:

"Ah, what is happening with you, dear? Why are you so thin?" Well here I'm getting to the point: she did not use the same heavy wording but simply elegantly declared "You should gain some weight—it would look nice on you as you are so tall!" She is, as they say, "a real lady", Serbo-Italian countess, so the rest of the evening she and her husband spent (noblesse oblige) teaching us the art of riding. She hated the French though and cherished bad souvenirs from France, somewhat like me, indeed! Unlike her though, I never mustered the courage to say "I'll never go back to France." My only attempt would consist making big plans to relocate myself to yet another country, then I make numerous trips to different places hoping I would remain in one forever.

Tomorrow happens to be our last day in Rome and I am wondering, really wondering how I will ever find strength to return to Paris?

Upon my return to Antonia's I almost found for myself a temporary solution; I threw a last glance at her gorgeous library (Kant, Nietzsche, Russell) and found in it a beautiful book, *Pasolini's Death* by Dario Bellezza.

This threw me right back to the only landscape where I truly belonged, the country where any real family of mine lived—of poets, writers, philosophers and artists. And it is not important really where I live as long as these people are directly or indirectly in my company. I remembered the man whom I called "my Italian husband" and who taught me to speak good Italian'whilst encouraging me to translate Sandro Penna, Dario Bellezza and Pasolini into Serbian, then into English. Bellezza says Pasolini "had a habit of risking his rare visions in some dark alley in a dubious suburb. He was taking the same risk as Verlaine and Oscar Wilde before him, or, the way Caravaggio took it, but many many centuries ago." Bellezza says wittily: "He was constantly trying to find a suicide on his escapades but what was awaiting him was plain murder." Pasolini said once "*Sono libero perché sono un po'più libero da me stesso.*" (I am free because I've managed to get rid of a tiny bit of me myself and I). Bellezza added that sex served both Pasolini and Nietzsche—just one purpose—to liberate them from overall misery and sadness… And Nietzsche resurrected in Pasolini to wake him up and remind him of his own hurt masculinity.

My trip to Rome was over.

part 2 VENICE
Carnival, February 2012

'The Concentration Camps were built
on architecture after the Grand Hotels'
(Alain Resnais in his film *Night and Fog*)

The encounter—both erroneous and fatal but undeniably spontaneous

I've read somewhere this idea of Resnais' and it occurred to me: if the concentration camps reminded the great director of the Grand Hotels, it is not so strange the Grand hotels in which I stayed a short time indeed resembled concentration camps and jails. But let's go back to those times when my unwilling and painful stays in big hotels started to take place.

I know you are likely to think I was pulling a number here, some dirty action "à la Stavisky" or a scam executed under some other great scammer's logo; however, as a street kid coming from a good family—I never truly dared to push any scam action to the point of the "Grand Hotel" profundity. In other words, and back in my early school days, I witnessed a wrong turn in certain supermarket products (mainly sweets and cosmetics) that crawled into my pockets instead of landing at the cashier's stand. But I never stayed in a hotel (or any place I rented) and then disappeared without paying the bill, no, I've never done that. It seems such action, suddenly disappearing from the hotel, was not even feasible nowadays, an era of computerised tourism, unlike the days of Al Capone or Stavisky. In my case, such action was not even necessary.

During my long life in Paris and that period covers almost three decades, I would occasionally meet with Louise, a hefty loud compatriot who had been raising five children from her different marriages, all alone. She lost track of the children's fathers. Louise was somewhat forced to use her own wits and employ different methods in order to feed her big family. In spite of circumstances, she managed to keep a certain grace and freshness in her spirit. Always she kept a natural broad smile on her face so that the people we knew were quite happy upon running into her and having any sort of brief exchange.

On the other side of the fence, I was that researcher cum writer and a scientist, interested in the mechanism of the oldest trade in the world, as well as the history of the social and political development of that trade was nothing but the history of poverty propelling or pushing women to exchange the most uninteresting hours of their life for some material gain. I was eager to know the elements of that particularly sad game of power. I wanted to know how exactly these women felt while spending their precious time with a client? I wondered what someone like Judy Butler would have to say to the situation in which she found herself, some neon-lit but dark sex shop in Pigalle, where such inhuman/human trade took place... Perhaps Louise would answer some of my questions. One particular day, when I was signing rather senselessly a stack of papers detrimental to my destiny and when I had sold my apartment due to an overall bankruptcy.

"Look here, it's going to be very simple," she exclaimed, as she was obviously cheered by my simple offer to come along and watch her performance. "Come along with me to the most exquisite restaurant *Pied du cochon*—I'm supposed to have dinner with an elderly gentleman who's afraid to dine alone. In fact, this extremely well-educated creep is not able to have sex with anyone but the portrait of his dead aunt who molested him when he was twelve. He himself is going to tell you all this once you get to know each other."

"Fine with me," I said, "and yet, I feel you should explain to your friend the purpose of my anthropological survey. It will really best serve my purely sociological and literary purposes."

Two hours later, Louise was applying heavy layers of powder over her cheeks in the toilet of the *Zin-Zin Bar*, alternating layers of make-up with cigarettes which she would light one after another: she was getting ready to enter the muddy waters of her profession. Once we downed a couple of cognacs, we walked to the renowned diner *Pied du Cochon*, and there in their lovely garden, a romantic gentleman in a white Panama hat waited for us leisurely stretched in the restaurant's green garden armchair. His face belonged to a certain viscount from, say, Chateaubriand's gallery of characters. He really did not belong to this century but rather an era prior. He kissed my friend's hand and then my own asking us politely to take a seat. One was bound to notice Louise's vulgar behaviour right away: she produced her camera and started taking endless pictures of the entire environment: she wanted first to frame the elegant waiters silently sliding from one table to another; then she would move the lens to the meals the waiters served while making loud comments like: "Look at that cake, Maximilian, gorgeous! Can you ask him to bring that cake over so that I might take a picture? No one is going to believe I ever entered a place like this!"

"I am only here to say hello and show you my new book," I joined the conversation awkwardly.

"So you are a writer, I assume." Jovial, the gentleman said while browsing the book rather casually until the title of a story caught his eye, *Baudrillard's Absence*.

All of a sudden he seemed very animated as if the title shook off his lazy slumber: "Have you ever met him in person?" He asked, then quickly, as if he was haunted by an afterthought, "He was a very good friend of mine, but as most of my dearest friends—he had to leave us early!"

I began telling him about the event upon which I met the great thinker, yes, of course, how could I ever forget the day I met such a person! Soon enough we began a very lively conversation to Louise's great chagrin who certainly did not expect such a turn of events during our small dinner.

By the end, Maximilian revealed that his real name was simply Claude, and I was to call him by that name from now on—and he had already thought up a great plan for all of us to meet again, say, in the beginning of the following week. He was to invite Louise and myself to the theatre! Two exquisite and bright ladies that we were, we had to decide on the show. He did not want to impose his particular taste on us. Louise was more than furious. I, a total debutant and charlatan, really going to snatch her best client from her? Human beings are so damn ungrateful—first you try to help a dire situation, explain what any job is about and the next thing you know, that debutant has snatched the job from you!

"Oh, come on, Louise, calm down," I tried to soothe her, "The guy just invited us to a theatre show… Louise, you don't think I would do… such a thing to a friend… ?"

Perhaps Louise felt she was in front of a huge gate forever closed to her, hiding an incredible garden full of unusual phenomena which included someone's absolute loyalty to my own creative processes. The loyalty expressed to me was not our friend's whim, on the contrary, it was a true, sincere and real emotion, which lasted for years and there was no one to ruin that friendship, one of the most important in my life and one of the most difficult to describe.

Claude Maximilian was a very wealthy philosophy teacher who was terrorised by the idea of dining by himself, and in order to prevent such complete terror he would invite the members of his extended family to join him for dinner in the most renowned restaurants of France.

His enclave of the most intimate friends, and I myself lucky enough to be part of that elite, he would take on numberless luxurious travels around the world. This group of selected friends—individuals of different colour and trade coming from all walks of life were entirely free to enjoy such travel as they pleased during the day—our only obligation consisted of meeting Maximilian at 8pm sharp every evening in the lobby of the hotel to have dinner with our gracious host—most likely the most renowned restaurants of the city. I tried to enjoy these travels as much as I could. Claude's friends were charming representatives of the French aristocracy or the upper middle class; girls like my friend Louise had no family upbringing to move within this group, thus I never encountered my friend in this context again.

My memories of these journeys have found their written form in various notes with the names of these grand hotels Resnais had named quite adequately as "the concentration camps."

February 1, 2012, Hotel Danieli, Venice

Claude is quite a significant philanthrope with a taste for luxury and an enormous affection for all his friends, and for me personally he is both *mecena* and a philanthrope. This time he took eight of us to Venice, more precisely to Danieli, a hotel without any stars to it and above ranking of that sort. However, God is my witness—I was afraid of traveling to that city. I was eight years old when I travelled the first time with my father to Venice. And then we travelled a lot to that city—dad and I, mother and I, were visiting aunt Olga, brother Gigi, wife Gilda. And there was Nino di Franco and other cousins, none of them I'd be able to locate in this city nowadays. Then my lovely honeymoon, then Olga's death in the hospital St. Angelo. A bunch of memories, whole loads of memories, burdens of memories falling over my shoulders, over my eyebrows, causing a constant flow of tears.

Well, here I am right now, sitting in the St. Vidal church listening to Vivaldi.

This church is the only quiet place in Venice, spared from the Carnival madness. All the people wear masks, bunch of tourists, hordes of crazies, to which my stomach turns so I didn't even get a chance to enter *Florian* where my dad and aunt took me to eat some special ice-creams. Lots of memories now, scads of tears. See what happens when one does not work things out in a therapy; it's a form of mourning never ended. I see right in front of me my different ages and seasons passing… I was five, ten, twenty-five then fifty-five—this is certainly the steepest, most profound journey into my interior. There is nothing to cry for, as there is nothing to cry about, we have to grow all of us, as I am doing it now, as we are all growing up until we die.

12/ 02/ 2012

It is clear to me why my aunt and grandma Rosa had always wanted to leave Venice in winter—they did not do it to avoid the surplus of rheumatism and this poisonous humidity. Also this water which penetrates bones and molecular cells. They would leave because of this feeling that I'm having right now, ever obliging to place yet another carnival mask over their face, already burdened by too many masks. The carnival mask was the real face of this city staggering under heavy masks, light effects, lampoons and costumes. Venice as such was a sort of theatrical creation, a sort of mad mask—so to place yet another mask, the carnivals' mask, was an exaggeration of Rococo mentality. An entropy of masks and an equally carnivalesque experience of this world. So in other words if I bought here a carnival mask it would be my third or forth. On my usual daily mask that I wear in Paris I had added the mask of Venice and over these two, I put the third, the mask of the Carnival itself! Come to think of it, the onion was a most sophisticated vegetable, and the Russian doll Matryushka maybe the best human toy of them all. Perhaps the carnival was the place everyone got an opportunity to peel his own layers and to face the hidden truths about himself and the surrounding world.

Let's go back through those people who once transformed this huge wax museum into the real capitol of the art world. These guys were Bellini, Tintoretto and Veronese who above all liked Turkish green and turquoise blue azure colors so no wonder I rushed to see these hues of the real Venetian sea splashing the walls of the city's Academy of Beaux Arts. In this building, half a century ago, I began writing my first childish impressions. The first thing I did today, in fact, was call Rosaria Ruffino but she was under the weather. She said she was not able to meet that afternoon, but strongly encouraged me to go to the Academy.

Here in the Academy and for the first time it happened that Veronese's take on the theme of the *Annunciation* appeared quite comical: his Angel appears as some stupid ballet dancer who made a silly *salto* through the air just to announce the happy news to the Virgin. The dove appears very aggressive, like a vulture, sort of, so the Virgin was scared of it—as if she were going to attack the lady with the Holy News. Bravo Veronese!

I reached Tintoretto's room filled with his baroque curves and creatures taking independent flights through the planes of his paintings. He almost reached abstraction on this one: *Madonna and her child, and the saints Cecilia,*

Marina, Cosma and Demian. Veronese presents himself as an utterly funny artist, with a huge sense of humor, whereas the vision of Gianbatista Tiepolo is deeply Baroque and fearsome. Was it really Tiepolo whom we could name as the first expressionist as his vision was full of snakes, gory events and scary faces?

In the Academy we are also likely to run into the chronicler of the Venetian dark chamber, Pietro Longhi, whose violinists were never less moving than say, Giorgione's *Old Woman.* What stirred my highest interest were Bellini's typically orthodox and Byzantine madonnas. There that famous painting *Virgin with the Red Cherub* which particularly interested Julia Kristeva which we discussed once together and which was also a sort of token of our friendship...

There was also Gentile Bellini's the *Miracle of the Relic from St. Laurentz's Bridge*, dating from 1429, a painting which terribly resembled a certain Pompeian fresco, but there was also the oldest Mantegna, *Saint George*, a part of the Academy's permanent collection. My gaze was taken by a gentle vision of Carlo Crivelli dating from 1430. It presented Saint Rocco and Saint Sebastian locked in a typically gay dream—the painter fell in love with a poor young idol posing for him in his ripped red stockings! There, right in Crivelli's vision we were to find the oldest of the Bellinis, Jacopo Bellini, whose tenderness was more overwhelming than the tender vision of his cousins: his Virgin with dropped and Oriental eyelids a sort of painting only accessible to poets. Carpaccio's *Arrival of the English Ambassadors* was a painting that rendered it to a sort of easier interpretation, thus a real joy for an innocent visitor.

I'd like to share something important with you here: my visit to the Academy not only dazzled my imagination it made me experience something totally new and unexpected—an experience which was a eureka moment for me: the old Sienna masters, like Vitore Carpaccio were getting inspiration for their work in the ancient Pompean frescoes; and not only that! The greatest Italian schools of painting were enriching themselves by the heritage of the old Roman antiquity—they also relied on the tradition of Byzantine fresco painting, at least that was what the Venetian art tradition was all about.

13/ 02/ 2012

I visited the Academy of Arts: simply magic. On Sunday, I was struck by a very bad sciatic pain, however. I could not budge an inch so I looked for the nearest pharmacy with Rachelita, Claude's oldest friend from Madrid, for some good three hours. Otherwise, Rachelita is the owner of the biggest literary agency in Spain and is used to helping poor authors especially poets. I managed to pull myself together.

Simonetta, the Roman, had taken us that afternoon to the rehearsal of *Cosi Fan Tutte* in La Fenice theater. It was an absolutely contemporary version of Donizetti's opera, but not the most brilliant so I forgot the name of the director. After the night at the opera we had that obligatory burgoise dinner with candles and the rest of the luxurious paraphernalia that in the most expensive restaurant in Venice. I assume that someone like Pasolini would not miss his chance to spit into one of the restaurant's plates. I went to bed and I slept a very long time; I do not remember any dreams but my sleep was long and nourishing. I woke up at 2pm the following day. A waiter brought me coffee to the room and inquired, "Are you alright, madam?"

Of course I'm alright. Perhaps I do not need special medications or additional analysis at this time. Perhaps I should just sleep better and longer from now on.

16/02/2012

Ca Resonico is a shiny palace of the Venetian *settecento* (18th century) with the ugliest Italian gallery of paintings one could ever imagine. *Ca Grimmani*, a Renaissance palace, on the contrary was one of the nicest buildings in the city and had been recently reconstructed. It shone in all its splendour. I saw there an incredibly beautiful painting by Hieronymus Bosch which reminded visitors that eternal purgatory as well as hell were stages awaiting us with impatience.

We visited St. Michele cemetery yesterday; the graveyard where exquisite people were buried: notably

Stravinsky. His friend and choreographer Daghliev, whose gravestone was decorated with a marble dance-shoe. Ezra Pound and Josef Brodsky were among the poets buried there. See what a poet's destiny was like—born in one country, a poet spends his life in another, to be buried in a third part of the world. All this seemed a topsy-turvy enterprise. In the afternoon I visited Pino foundation and the Guggenheim, as well as the Palazzo Grassi where Francesco Vezzoli, a new hope in contemporary Italian art, was giving a conference in front of three hundred people who all looked like stuffed puppies and kittens, their attitudes very similar to Jeff Koons's.

Where is Contemporary Art heading now?

To disaster? To certain disaster and a new anti non entity?

The cemetery was quiet though, and pensive as Stravinsky and Daghliev, Pound and Brodsky took their rest.

That particular evening I saw Rosaria Ruffino, a teacher of avant garde theater who wrote her doctoral thesis on Peter Brook and presented it at la Sorbonne. She took me to a Renaissance concert which took place in the Association of Musicians of Venice whose headquarters were in one of the city's ruined palaces under eternal construction. As we were listening to the endless madrigals of Adriano Banchieri and Marco Uccellini, I completely understood that Venice has never abandoned the mentality of the seventeeth century; that is why one could still find in one of its numerous music shops and studios instruments whose perfect sound and fabrication were worth that of a Stradivarius.

Soon we found all the members of Claude's joyful company and chat casually in the legendary salon of the Danieli hotel. Claude, Rosaria, Cincia and Simonetta were all in a very relaxed casual mood and the perfect Martini, cold flowing like a river down our throats. That particular dining-room will always remain my best memory—not because of exquisite silver or luminous crystal lamps which decorate its corners, but of an incredible quantity of French verses I translated in that room. This is exactly what has befallen me: anytime I walk into that room an unexpected influx and surge of concentration comes to me, some invisible force prompted me to read and write and which I believe completely disappeared from my busy Parisian life. Every morning, while co-travelers were still asleep, I would sneak into this salon and translate contemporary French poets, but with such abandon and rapidity that had been escaping my mind for years that I did not even feel the urge to take a dictionary with me to consult the expressions normally obligatory for a professional. Words which sort of haunted me, flowing in and out of my brain would come as separate entities, I observed their flow, rejoiced at the new phenomena until one day... An elderly waiter approached discretely and placed a casual cup of cappuccino on my table: "*Signora,* I noticed you have been writing something for days here, but do you know that Georges Sand and Alfred de Musset had also lived here, just like you, and legend has it that they would also come to this room early in the morning in order to write."

I felt quite grateful to him for this revelation. Much later, I learned that Wagner wrote the greater part of *Tristan and Isolde* in this very room.

February 18, 2012.

All of a sudden very warm here as we decided to do our sightseeing on a local boat, *vaporetto*, early this morning—our destination was the local island of Murano, famous for its glasswork. The glass beads and numerous gilded figurines produced a certain nausea in Claude, so the two of us decided to return quickly to the city. As we were crossing the Rialto Bridge, Claude confessed he knew that all the glass jewelry and clothes meant very little to me, Nina the writer. He thought up a nicer event, a personal gift, was going to present it to me that very evening. Allegedly he invited all our travelling companions, even my friend Rosaria to the legendary bar, *Harry's*, where Hemingway wrote his entire novel *The Old Man and the Sea*. I have always felt intuitively the Venetian sea put a special spell on Hemingway as much as on Thomas Mann because it was Venice where they started writing the processes of ageing and dying.

There was something in this turquoise sea

enveloped in fog that prompted writers to plunge into contemplation.

That very afternoon had the honor to meet Gabriele, an anarchist and leading member of the Italian left who belonged, back in 1968, to the virulent branch of the movement *Potere operaio (Power to the Workers)*. Gabriele met me in a small bar near the marvellous edifice of St. Rocco Church and repeated the same story Rosaria had told me three days ago. The municipality of Venetto has always been a left-oriented republic, to the point that Venetians are said to be the only Italians who threw tomatoes and eggs at Berlusconi when he showed in Venice to collect votes.

From 1993 to 2009 the mayor of Venice was a Marxist philosopher Massimo Cacciari. During his long term governing he really proved that a philosopher was a being qualified for the task. All the citizens had a great respect for him, even his enemies from the opposite party. I remembered here the testimony of the philosopher Mihailo Markovich who told me once he had the same dream for Serbia, to be governed by philosophers. He ended up though at Milosevich's court and we all know how his career ended. Cacciari's destiny was much better, although he was not able to achieve that total fiscal autonomy for Italian cities. I hear Markovich's voice emerging from the background: "It must had been easier for Cacciari to contemplate the future of the state in that unusual Venetian pinkish and turquoise light than it was for me, alongside Mr. Miloshevic!"

And what would have happened, ever, to our Serbian artists and history if our painters applied Markovich's analogous reasoning to their work? What if they could have just said that it was useless for them to work since they were never destined to achieve Bellini's greatness, who did not really have to work hard, nor Tintoretto, Titian nor Veronese for that matter—all these great artists being born into Venetian colors which one could never master otherwise.

If they only dared say the Venetians are born with an easel and that learning does not improve arts!

February 20, 2012

I overslept and missed our visit to Torcello, the oldest Venetian island. I felt terribly tired after being awake for half a hour. As it happened to be the last day of my trip, I wanted to see even a tiny corner of beloved Venice lit by the moring light. And it was Venice the *serenissima* and not I that morning.

I am supposed to leave for Paris from the airport this very evening, but before I finally pack my suitcase and check out from this legendary hotel I want to visit Wagner's house. Or more precisely the place where he lived for a year and where he died on February 13, 1883.

Soon enough I found myself in front of palazzo *Ca Vendramin Calergi*, built in the 15th century. The building had changed through several aristocratic owners before it became the property of the unfortunate duchess de Berry, who confined the palace to Wagner that particular winter in which he died. Today, the lower floor of the palace houses a casino, and on its upper floor—where the father of the Avant-garde used to live—the Wagner Society opens its doors to Wagner's suite for visitors who observe with a somewhat religious scrutiny the room where the great composer passed out bent over the piano. Before his life ended in this palace, Wagner had always stayed in Danieli hotel, more precisely throughout November 1861 and October 1880. He loved Venice because of the water which will eventually swallow the city and because of that huge mental space Serenissima used to give to her passers-by.

I barely missed the building—it was so difficult to find my way. On that particular day the streets were crowded and cramped with creatures attending the Carnival and everyone yelled the loudest they could. I found myself on the Rialto bridge and got stuck on it for hours and I could not move left nor right but finally made my way to *Ca Vendramin*. Wagner's bedroom was almost empty. Every corner of that room was able to show a tiny particle of his very own particular magic, a tiny lamp next to his pillow which emanated very soft light, as in a dream.

The room was stuffed with artificial but perfumed roses which probably didn't do any good to the already damaged composer's frail health. The central part of the room was occupied by a very big canape covered with a brocade tissue. I had a feeling Wagner simply rested on that couch a short interval, somewhat like me, he must had been scared by big beds and the sudden appearance of the Angel of Death.

In his bedroom, both intimate and impersonal a door led to another which was central to this suite and had in its middle a huge black animal, Wagner's pianoforte covered by silk. And on top of it the same fake roses with their unbearable faded scent. I wondered, when he fell over the piano playing his last score, at a time when his *anima suspiria* was leaving, which melody was the last to part with him?

Jacques Rancière was right: music is not only a certain art. It is something higher than that. It is a certain idea about art and as Wagner's favorite, Schopenhauer remarked, above all it is an idea within anti-representation. It has always been, as it is today, the art which speaks loudly about emotions that go beyond forms of identification, simple situations and visible representation. It is an art of the unnamable as well as an art of the unspeakable. And it penetrates us in a way we are not given to describe.

SPAIN

(Sevilla)
THE ALFONSO XIII HOTEL

May 5, 2011.

The Alfonso XIII hotel is a palace built in Neo-Mudehar style and was built next to Alcazar, in Seville, Andalusia. It was exactly where Claude and I and his tiny group of friends landed one bright sunny morning. Who were all these illustrious people I was supposed to share the following few days in this gorgeous, luxurious atmosphere? The purpose of the trip was to attend Grand Feria—the grand festival of bullfights which is the biggest ethno-cultural event in Spain since 1847 which their glorious Queen Isabella had started. And the festival has been going on ever since, in the sunny and quiet town of Seville which many consider the cradle of the bullfight.

This time around, the group of friends whom Claude invited to keep him company consisted of the psychoanalysts living in different countries who were willing, above all, to watch corrida on a daily basis. They were also willing to admire young girls in Spanish lace and the Seville costumes—in order to conclude oh, yes, they all agreed on this one- that these girls were more beautiful than El Greco's *Virgin* in the local cathedral. In my view, these girls were no better than flamenco Gypsy music and dance, which ruled Seville unofficially. These have also been the symbol of the Arabic soul still very present in the region.

Will they ever be capable of understanding this simple truth, this particular group of the *Grand bourgeoisie* ever so different from one another and at the same time condemned to be so much alike?

The remarks they were making about one another I failed to like from the beginning of the trip. And that was when I had written that the greatest tragedy for someone is to speak many languages as a consequence is so that, easily, people can understand everything said around him! And I was not witty, as say, our friend Oscar Wilde!

But let's see who our friend Claude really was? He was quite refined and tender. He was cruel and oblivious in his ignorance as he sometimes lacked the basic knowledge of human character. His friendship, his care for his friends over exceeded the usual notion of philanthropy as we often found ourselves bedazzled by his actions.

Dr. Hausser, my French analyst, thinks he is a man who does not know what to do with his money. And that is true. He is both perplexed and scared by the process of ageing and one possibility he would have to dine alone just once in his lifetime. So he invited a team of ten different friends to attend Feria. They have to eat cakes and watch bulls killed by matadors every five minutes. When an exhausting day with Claude and his Feria events is over, I still find time to visit the flaming flamenco clubs in Seville and read my books on Transactional analysis so that I might calm my mind.

May 6, 2011.

The facial expression of the Andalusians here is calm, and subdued—all the girls resemble my sister in-law Emma; and all the boys look like Marc, my son's father. The old men resemble Pepe Jo, my father-in-law! They hail from this part of the world. There's a proverb attests to my observation that says "blood differs from water" as it stays flowing in men's bloodstreams for generations, thus it marks people in a very peculiar way. I am sad to admit I was not marked by family blood in any given way; my brother turned 78 yesterday but I am not in possession of his moral strength nor energy, nor do I have that proverbial stamina of the Zivancevic family.

Last night I collapsed having watched the bullfights, then visit to the Alcazar followed by a short walk through the city. All this, in fact, a great stress imposed on my system—the visit to the region where my ex-husband's family came from. And a great part of me was truly curious to learn the customs and mentality of the people with whom I shared a part of my life in France. I wanted to fathom the ethnic reasons, if there were such an anthropological thing, of the strange behavior of my husband's family, who were both cruel and sturdy but somewhat tender and emotional.

It seemed to me I have almost understood the complexity of their strange mentality by observing the insane and cruel, almost infantile, rigid activity of the corrida. It did not appeal to me as sport or game but appeared more like a cruel and infantile competition between man and a bull who does not have a choice. A senseless animal, condemned to death from the start. Come to think of it, that is also a matador's fate. It appears to me as action equaling action—a senseless boy who hangs a cat by its tail and suffocates it over the fiery flames. The final grace here arrives in the end after *picadors* challenge the bull, piercing his back with *picas* (spikes). The bull keeps bleeding incessantly, overlooking the golden and pink cape of the matador, this last teases the bull by calling "hay, hay." The matador's action reminds me in fact of the family behavior of my ex-husband, but the matador appears more graceful here as he finally pierces the bull with his sword and liberates him from further suffering.

However, he takes hours to finish with the bull and during these long hours of a bull's agony the matador keeps teasing the wounded until the bull finally drops. And before the audience gets exhausted from cheering and hand-clapping (remember, the matadors are doing all this in order to gain attention from the audience). Finally they arrive at the final stage of the game when the matador executes a *coup d'grace* and after that final blow—a more gallant part follows with ladies throwing hats and fans into the arena, the matadors kiss these objects and throw them back to the ladies…

From two matadors who we saw in action yesterday, the elder performed his job more seriously: he took off his shoes and bare-feet, entirely covered with the bull's blood, he approached the dying animal. He risked his personal security and embraced the animal that weighed some 538 kilograms. I think his name was Miguel; the younger one, Narcisso, was quite handsome, as his name indicates. He appeared self-assured but in a hurry to get to that final stage of the spectacle, the exchange of hats and fans which he was to kiss and return. I threw him my hat as well, but he did not return it so I had to chase the guards and the cleaners of the arena afterward begging them to return it to me.

Even the act of watching the bullfights is a very tiring process. I wonder as to what kind of emotional vacuity and depravity causes people to indulge in this sport. I know this much: many authors and artists whom I truly admired happened to like Tauromachy a great deal: the writers such as Hemingway and Michel Leiris, and the artist Picasso, for example. My taste was somewhat different as I faced death during my lifetime. This particular way of coming close to it did not appeal to me—I found this approach banal and obvious, and somewhat less than educational…

The most interesting part of our stay here was a visit to the royal palace of Alcazar where Queen Isabella sent Columbus to America. Here, from her own window nested in the midst of a wing overlooking the garden, the Queen watched a bush of her favorite bougainvillea while ruling the whole planet. So this palace, as a particle of universe as much as Andalusia, the tiniest corner of the globe have been a symbol of the encounter the different worlds and a symbol of inner cohesion as well. The respective worlds of Arab, Spanish, Christian, Jewish and Moslem origins. Seville has served as the symbol of the art of translation of these different cultures one into another. Thus you find that ever wise and at the same time tender and comprehensive expression of character in the face of all Andalusians (or the Vandalusians, as the Arabs who conquered Southern Spain in 711 used to call the people in "the land of the vandals"). And the Alcazar, one of the nicest landmarks of this land, is marked by that strange mixture of sweetness and relaxed atmosphere that belongs to the climate.

May 8, 2011.

It is a cold day and it rains, a persistent rain that belongs to Seville. In fact, Spaniards represent the epitome of bullfights, the adoration of Christ, the constant flow of blood and their deadly passion—here we have the constant encounter between Eros and Thanatos. The bullfight in this sense is an erotic sport, an erotic experience as the very act of piercing the bull with a sword is followed by torrents of blood and the dance of the *matador* around his deadly target a dance of the lover who has seduced the bull.

This is something I have always failed to understand. Yes, I say never, until today, when I had visited the small and beautiful museum with the paintings of Zurbaran, and Valdes de Leal, Murillo. Their representations of Christ presented the bull who was loved, passionately adored, then tortured and covered with blood.

All of this is called Spanish Baroque or Passion and indeed there is no better city than Seville to show these works in all their intensity. In these museums we find IT: that very Spanish quality which is the baroque quintessence of Baroque. This certain quality belongs solely to Seville and is a rare quality. Here we have Christianity mixed with Arab culture, so Christian civilization is quite oriental, enriched with a Byzantine flavor—the same goes for my home town, Christian and Turkish, that is, it maintains an Oriental calm and is contemplative, an inheritance from the Ottomans.

May 10, 2011.

It is going to be a beautiful day. I could not say I recognize the day because the morning happens to be so beautiful because I overslept and woke very late again. I sleep so well in this soft and super-luxurious hotel Alfonso XIII, where a fish meal costs one hundred euros!

I take a shower and walk lazily downstairs to have breakfast, with a boring book on Transactional analysis, and my diary in a big folder. I usually eat yoghurt and fruit waiting for some miracle to happen, a medieval *miraculum*, and that miracle is simply a sudden outburst of spontaneous energy. Then I try to make a plan: How to give some creative meaning to my day which usually lasts from 10am until 4pm, that is, until we meet, eight of us fellow-travelers and Claude, in the hotel's lobby so we can all fit into one huge taxi to take us to the local arena the *Plaza del Torros*: Bull's Square where we are to attend the afternoon session of bullfights. During the whole of the past week (see how time flies!) I was doing my best to fill my free time, noon until 4pm, and to see the best of what Seville could offer, then to pick the best impressions of Claude and fellow-travelers. Happy little creature that I was, I constantly have a feeling that in one of my previous lives I was Spanish and had lived here. It was strange to me that out of all other possibilities in my life to come and see Seville, I ended up as a prisoner in a five star hotel!

There was not a trace of animosity towards our generous host, Claude, and how could there be? His entire lifestyle, his wealth, his peculiar friendships, did appear extremely odd. I will try tomorrow, one more time—and this the last moment before we return to Paris—I will try to fathom the real reason for Claude's strange existence.

I tried to fathom it even today during breakfast hour, but my endeavor did not bring any results. I arrived to the dining room this morning, five of his friends already helping themselves to breakfast, at the same time making very loud plans where to spend the evening. None of them knew anything about Claude, say nothing more than order through a waiter serving us for the occasion. Except for Raquelita, his friend from Madrid who used to know Claude's father, eh, but this woman was extremely silent, discreet and subdued—the adjectives here are well applied. An introvert who would not allow anyone to untangle intricate secrets.

That very evening old Claude had taken terrible umbrage with me—I mentioned something related to his father, and our host became so furious with me, I swear I have never seen anyone that furious in my entire long life! His rage lasted two minutes, but it was so big, enormous that its flames could have burnt the entire palace of Alcazar in two seconds!

A few hours later our friend Jean Max, a professional psychologist, took some time to explain the source and origin of this rage.

Here is the account of what really happened: I had a couple extra drinks at the table and I felt quite irritated by Sylvia's behavior. This Italian friend of Claude's did not waste time constantly complaining through false modesty, criticizing everyone's habits. She did not fail to mention that 'unlike everyone else, she herself hated bullfights, that she was a vegetarian and a real humanist' etcetera etcetera. At a certain moment I felt compelled to ask her that final question which served Margo, my friend and the oldest drag queen in New York City, to end any unpleasant dinner or an unrewarding friendship:

"And what did your father do during Mussolini's (or rather Hitler's) era?"

I remember Claude's face turned deep grey green. If these two colors were poetically adequate to describe Claude's trauma which materialized at that particular moment, I'm not sure Jean Max described my question as "way too personal," one of those which certainly went too deep and too far into Claude's family history.

What can I tell you? This question which I asked Sylvia did not cause the ending of the trip in any radical manner—the voyage was already laced with conversational undertones and, anyway, it was meant to end the following day.

ENGLAND

(LONDON)
Savoy Hotel, 2011,2012, 2013

Claude and I (once he declared me one of his most intimate friends) stayed in the Savoy Hotel on several occasions. As I have been thoroughly acquanted with London and lived there before, I knew a lot of people there, so during these three-week trips I was never long at the hotel. I would return to the Savoy only to change my wardrobe (It always seemed somewhat lifeless and impersonal.) Bob Dylan certainly did not share with me this opinion as they say that he exceptionally treasured this hotel and some of the his nicest songs were composed there. Yes, it has been the lodging place for a number of musicians but it was too impersonal for my taste, one of those places where you drop your suitcase and run out to do business. I remember on several ocassions I would leave my keys to some of my less fortunate friends who would come to London from distant parts of the globe, but who had no place to stay. I would usually stay with my Goran in Stockwell and would would go to the Savoy only to take a swim in the pool reserved for the special guests, and use the sauna facilities afterwards. Here I'd like to add something about my last stay in the hotel:

2013. I was not honestly looking forward to visiting again this most beautiful *manor* built by the tallest and the thinnest John the Gaunt in the thirteenth century, as we were lodged the previous year in some shabby rooms destined to the king's horsemen on the first floor in a forlorn and neglected part of the hotel. This time things seemed different. Claude, our *mecene*, seemed more than happy that I, who was never on time, appear finally on time at the Parisian station Gare de Nord. It was five o'clock in the morning and our Eurostar in the direction of London was steaming and neighing like a good horse. In fact, I'm just joking: the train was inaudable.

DIBUK

We reached the Savoy hotel at Strand and I was led to the fourth floor in the traditional part of the hotel, more precisely suite 409 where madame Marie Marguerite Fahmy on July 10, 1923 fired her gun and killed her husband, the Egyptian prince Ali Kamel Fahey Bey. In the end of the text which was to be read underneath of the photograph of this lady whose face was the epitome of sadness, I could read that "she was finally acquitted by the court at the Old Bailey". As if it really mattered what happened. And what had in fact happened?

Why did this young, extremely beautiful woman, French, of catholic upbringing, kill the young Egyptian prince who from his earliest days, used to munch Turkish delights while abusing little boys or animals? In what harem cum trap had she found herself, this woman with such sad eyes and bitter, clenched lips, standing in thin robe, fingers covered in jewels as depicted in the photo? Such rage leading her to a well-planned murder. Instigated by her discovery of some awful secret she had been evading for years....or she discovered the prince's secrets in due time but took a forever to figure how to avenge. Yes, she had to kill, and Agatha Christie was just like a baby ideologist for her here, at the moment when Marie Marguerite Fahmy realised her desire, which turned into the very action—*passage à l'acte*—as the

French would call it. How was I to sleep in that room, I wondered. I was bound to find some other suite. I called and asked a young concierge to find me another suite.

The concierge agreed and noticed I had my violin with me. He offered to place me in a more musically oriented part of the hotel. There, just accross the apartment of that unfortunate Madame Fahmy an old suite where Maria Callas used to stay. He indicated the difference in price, so great that I immediately stopped contemplating my transfer to yet another suite.

I would return to that doomed suite and I play my violin there—to calm the ghosts, if any left from the 1920s. I would start with the scores from Glück's opera *Orpheus and Euridice.* I played part of the score appropriately intitled *Blessed Ghosts.* I felt some special music would calm them. Whoever remained and whoever may still dwell behind the thick window-curtains.

After that I called up my London friends.

Boyana, the Egyptologist. A beautiful and truly smart daughter of the former president of Yugoslavia. Somewhat under the weather she had recently become injured by the vile behavior of one of her closest cousins. I listened to her story, as if I were her true sister, and indeed I have been.

We lived in the same quarter in New York but never got to see each other properly. Now I'd say for the first time, in London, I've come to understand her archeological messages that contain a certain political background. Whatever she had to say—she was right.

Beau, my ex-husband, sat with cats in his apartment in Portobello Road ever thinking what was he to do in London. To do or not to do. All of us here represented part of those lost generations nowhere to fit in and nowhere left to go. He has been fighting the dragons of the British administration for quite a while and now it appeared unbecoming, a true Serbian intellectual, to bear the burden of bureaucratic plight. So how did we find ourselves in this boiling cauldron of life in Western Europe, all of us, when the cauldron has been boiling with mistrust and misunderstanding of the spiritual, Christmas decorations included, with its glittery pompous empty snowflakes?

And how it all went by so quickly! Our youth, so quickly, I thought while sitting on the couch like Edith Sitwell in a Victorian salon, on the fourth floor of the Savoy where Madame Fahmy killed her Egyptian prince.

"You know," I told Beau later that afternoon, "you were so lucky to have missed that heavy Murano ashtray I threw at you that day. If it *had* landed on you... it would have killed you."

"Ah, that particular day. I was so close to the brim of abysmal destiny... but I was so much younger and my reflex quicker than it is today."

He was sitting in a Victorian chair in the lobby of the hotel, smiling that kind, good-natured smile of his, full of surprise and wonder—the expression of his I knew so well.

Much later, we all joined Claude for dinner, nine of us in that incredibly priceless however bad restaurant. As we respected Claude and his invitations, no one dared indicate the food was horrible. I was tired and tried not to fall asleep at table.

The very following day, Claude and I set out for Orpington, a place in Greater London where he went to advance his language studies as a thirteen-year-old boy. The taxi driver had taken us to this suburb of Kent now showing us around, proud enough to declare the small town has developed significantly from the time when Claude was there. Claude did not find the house he lived in.

I tried to visit the house where I was born at, the Topchider Hill in Belgrade, but everything in that area was so changed I could not recover from that visit for days after. The old house still stood, but everything was so changed that it seemed that was *not* the place I was born. It must have been elsewhere...

London is one of those rare places where I always *feel* young, as if I spent a good part of my youth and childhood here. And I probably did. Once, when I was a student, my father came to look for me when I was squatting the studio of Mikki Moulton in Camden. And on another occasion, Beau and I walked through the city for days looking for the apartment. We did not find it. He himself found it much later, but with Grace, on Portobello Road, where he's been with his cats ever since.

Grace recently passed away. It is Christmas eve tonight and I am not going to leave Beau all alone. Beau has never mortally betrayed me. Perhaps he betrayed me once, it was not high treason though—but after that we stopped living together.

What could one qualify as betrayal? It often comes out as an inconguency of desire, incompatibility of feeling or action—like the times when I wished to have children. Beau did not want them, so the very desire to have children was sort of betrayed. These were old stories—youth gone and I found myself wrting a book dedication to my son's father: "To the only man who never betrayed me by proving love is something *more* than a four-letter word."

January 7, 2013.

An extremely pleasant afternoon with Inga and playwright-composer Johnny Brown. They are definitively in the group of friends who've never deceived. I invited them for lunch, together with Beau, to the Savoy. Johnny is full of new creative ideas, as usual, and within that scope invited Beau and I to be his guests on his radio show the following Friday. My friend Lela will arrive from Belgrade tomorrow—it would be good if I could persuade Claude to sponsor our theatre performance we are working on, and, how about if we invited him to be on the radio as well? Claude declined our offer in a very awkward way. It seemed to me he was the one who had the most interesting things to say:

well, we tried to persuade him. It did not work and then we left him alone, or rather with his friends to dine in peace. The journalist Monique and her husband, the psychologist Jean Max were the nicest out of his crowd. We said hello and good-bye and left the Savoy for the small and charming cafe *Charles Dickens.*

The Almighty is my witness that writers such as Dickens, Zola and Hugo have always meant to me more than Edith Sitwell, Oscar Wilde...and the rest of the visitors to the Savoy.

January 9, 2013.

My violin sounds beautiful in this part of the hotel, especially the British composers Elgar and Handel. One could see they composed in this part of the country and under such climate: I play their scores now to my visitors, especially to Niall, and all my friends agreed I have to practise more. The unrehearsed music was better here than say the firing of a gun—and it was certainly better at quieting those remaining ghosts. Niall and I took a long walk to the Serpentine, a place in itself full of good ideas, just like my friends Johny Brown and James Byrne, all poets *par excellence.* They all have asked if they had been properly dressed to enter the hotel, as if their incredible minds were not good enough to provide entrance to this material paradise. I do my best to convince them they would be left alone here, no one will threaten their existence, we are just surrounded with poodles of Capitalism, their bellies full and their heads full of stockmarket quotes. Niall is an Irishman and a Celt, of Celtic origin, he is always inclined to love a good drop of alcohol—so his task consists of dropping by early every morning—a visit which would leave my small fridge and room-bar empty. All these bottles of champagne, whisky, blue vodka would end up in his bag. I guess he decided to keep them through winter. I guess he needs to make himself warm.

January 10, 2013

Lela has finally arrived in London, with her daughter Milena, but has a terrible cold. I give her my magnet-key so they can stay in the suite while I am off to Paris where I have to take care of affairs and my own apartment. I was eager to return to London, and in fact I was rushing to get back to London although my back was strained and I could not move much. But I was rushing, as if I had a foreboding that my final hour awaited me in Paris, together with some casual friends there.

I dreamt some horrible and heavy dream: I was living in Paris and meeting friends from the Muppet show, Myriam and Aspasia. They would have sold me for a penny, or perhaps for some chunkier lump of money, say fifteen cents.

I was rushing to get back to that cosy little nest in the Savoy where my violin sounded the way those arpeggios in my youth did, when I played them softly.

In Paris I had lunch with Vladi who is always in need of my presence. He decided to come to London on Monday evening—I always have to be there for him whenever he needs his mother. My own mother was negligent in that respect, but I'm not, I cannot be that way—no, *not I, not I..* (Samuel Becket). So I bought him a ticket and a lot of dispute with my awful bank, however, but found some money and on top of it all, I found the best baclavas for Beau. Then I packed everything in a tiny suitcase and jumped on a train, my back hurting, and returned to London.

Lela and I spent the whole morning calling numbers to all sorts of theater houses. She's taking care of her Milena the way I take care of Vlad—in other words, she's my real family.

She *is* my real sister and not someone else, yes she is. We finally got tickets for *Master and Margarita*, a theatre play which I described to young Milena as a piece where a man has to decide between the act of having lunch with God or dinner with the Devil.

And Milena retorts with a question "And how am I to know who is the Almighty and who's the Devil when I see these gentlemen?"

She understood everything. She is such an incredibly bright, mature child.

14/01/ 2013.

The Serbian New Year...:

The real New Year's party started two days ago when I invited Ranka to the hotel. Ranka is chatty and a silly friend of mine from bygone days. She takes lots of drugs but she knows how to behave. Needless to say, Claude took a great liking to her. I wanted an ally in this hotel, I needed someone who would quiet this provincial French crowd; that crowd does not speak any foreign language but has a lot of complexes and is altogether racist.

Here comes Ranka though to give me a hand and shows up at the right moment when I have finally lost patience, with them and with Claude. The latter started imposing a bunch of nebulous requests like the one that arrived early at my door. He woke me at 7am, an emergency call, as he was all dressed and ready to see Karl Marx's grave at the Highgate Cemetry. We took a taxi-cab to Highgate and the cab driver took less than two hours to clean his nails while waiting for us to return to the car. Well, Claude took two hours to see the grave of Karl Marx. He did not pay particular attention to the grave Alma Mahler, the unfortunate composer's wife, whose grave was located next to Marx's. No, he did not have to say I was the only person among his crowd of friends who considered this place holy. I mentioned that I considered Alma's grave a holy place but Claude's disinterest in music did not approve of such an opinion. Claude and Karl Marx! Can you imagine!

Last night I had a visit from the poet and a musicologist David Miller. We started talking and drinking and the visit turned into a big drinking bout. Now while sobering, I was getting the message clearly: I am not going to have drinking bouts here or anywhere: the binges are detrimental to my health, detrimental to the general atmosphere and detrimental to this shapeless form of being which took such a long time to blossom. My only desire has been, ever since I a child, to meet my true inner being, my better self—and alcohol prevents me from achieving that final goal. So I should get rid of it!

My Vladi is about to arrive, my only child, so everything is supposed to get better. He does not belong to this stupid, retarded crowd where everyone eats and drinks and sleeps, suffering their own inner boredom. These are characters he has nothing to do with, the kid even said once jokingly "Mom, I am not going to be a bohemian like you!" So what is he likely to become, I wonder? At any rate, he is not going to be like Beau, stuck in a local foodstore buying catfood for his pets while waiting for a delivery of drugs from his Pakistani dealers.

The snow starts falling. It is Serbian New Year's day but it does not feel like a beginning of a new year nor the beginning of a new era. It feels like the ending of a very tiring and tiresome period.

I was lucky to have taken my violin, my only friend.

It is unjust and unfair of me to say so—my boyfriend Goran has just called a minute ago! It is totally unclear to me why I have spent an entire week in London and I haven't seen him yet!

*PARIS—
LIMA, PERU*

June 20, 2013

It was one of those rare voyages I took without Claude. He desired it so much and was slowly dying as he was deprived of it; at the same time he despised it and had a feeling that the very word suffocated him, even the very notion of it, the very idea to see it in print was driving him mad. I am talking about poetry, of course, which is my breath of life and for Claude. It was the worst torture to bear that one had invented in this universe. No, of course not—we were not meant to travel together for any professional reasons. However, I myself was not ready to set out on any journey whatsoever. I was swallowed up by the projects which I had not even time to start considering and those included some professional writings that were supposed to get done a while ago. One of those papers was meant to go to Serbia, it was old and sitting on my table for a month, predestined to ornate the monography of one of my best friends who disappeared quite early from our young, artistic lives. It read: "I've been looking at the drawing, Gera's drawing "*Long Story Man*" when the day when we first met came back to me. He was sitting with Giulia in their E. 5th Street apartment in New York when Carlos Stephanos and I showed up. I don't remember if it was a sunny or a rainy day, the climate or season in fact did not matter to us. The vertical movements of his brush accentuated the verticality of his figure- he was inviting everyone to some vertical adventure, however—and I was to discover all this much later in Paris—only he and I were capable of thinking about art… that much VERTICALLY."

I took that scrap of paper with me and a bunch of books with me. Lima seemed to be the city in which the memories thicken then sit well then disappear all of a sudden. The trip started with a funny, jovial adventure. Pierre Merej was dragging my broken second hand suitcase behind him towards Porte de Clichy where I was to take a train to the Orly airport. I was happy as a lark due to the fact that I had exactly 168 hours (7 days times 24 hours) devoted to reading, writing and to all sorts of processes which enlarge or even tighten our spiritual horizons, in an unknown landscape, physically gratifying and lush (the Bolivar hotel in Lima), luxurious but at the same time discreet and unimposing… where all my colleagues would either love me or hate me, where these international fellow-poets would respect me while being either jealous or admirative of my work…And the last but not the least—where I will not spend my creative hours listening to the banging of the hammer or the squealing sound of my neighbors' drill, those folks who live on the seventh floor of our noisiest Parisian building on boulevard Ney…

Pierre gave me a significant ally's wink when I told him this story (he wanted to indicate that some incredible marvels and adventures awaited on this particular journey).

I played Bach's "Aria" for him before leaving the apartment (after one year of rehearsing this heavy peace, will I be able to decipher it finally?)

Vlad has been filling my thermos with coffee and Pierre was listening to Bach attentively while spitting at the administration system of Bucharest where he visited last year when a tiny, quite thin ray of light penetrated my room and stayed in there lingering over my entire life.

All of a sudden I did not feel lost and lonely. My protective pendulum in gold and turquoise colors hanging from my neck was turning left and right—I started thinking that even the most elusive things in life—such as friendship and love could come back to us, there was a possibility.

Apparently, I had some old friends, even in the city of Lima; there was my old friend Indran, poet from New York and an Indian, who said he was waiting for me there—with impatience. I survived my changing of several different airports, changing different capacities of respiration on board of various planes (airs) and after some good nineteen hours to and through Madrid and forth, we finally arrived in Lima.The airport was a real American one, with long lines of passengers waiting for the passport control. The airport resembled a bad version of the abandoned and forlorn customs offices. I was surprised to find here a shabby imitation of the North American patterns of rules and regulations. And here, while waiting in a line for the passport check-up, I wrote the following poem:

A Letter from a Simple GUA (human being)

I am a simple Gua,
While moving and breathing
On my way from Trujillo to Lima,
I see a python,
I see a flower and I see the face of the last Inka emperor
Who's dying of scorbutic and of human lice in Lima…
I will never sit down
And I will never take a rest because
The very word "Gua" means "a being
who-never-sits-down",
If I sit down then I will die,
And I am here on Earth just in order to learn
How we could save all the forests
And how to save the forestian being "Gua"
Who we find in these forests…

The customs officer gave me exactly ten days to stay in Peru; this much I asked from him and he gave me precisely what I had asked him to give—he was not quite generous and that's quite alright. Ten days is exactly what I need to read some texts in Spanish and eventually write a poem, as I am that Gua, that human being constantly on the move.

The Peruvian organizers of the festival were waiting for our delegation at the airport. It was winter there, a cold July morning in Lima. They tried and managed successfully to place the three of us, a woman poet from Colombia and her boyfriend, a poet from Sweden and then me—into a large taxi cab rather quickly. I do not know how to take this overall and exaggerated care on the side of the organizers as it goes a bit over the notion of the basic care on the part of the organizers of such poetry festival and I am just a simple Gua. As if I was to become aware of an imminent danger which some of my friends tried to convey to me before I started this trip—and these were my buddies who travelled a lot through the Latin American countries. They all agreed in one thing- that human life did not have a very high price in these lands, it was even less important than in some African countries where no one felt quite safe, "You should never leave your hotel by yourself Nina, not even to buy cigarettes," they adamantly argued with me on that particular issue…

I myself am quite a reasonable and sensitive GUA, so I did not even have to listen to my friends' numerous warnings about the Latin continent; it was enough for me to enter that huge Peruvian lobby of their colonial hotel and to feel its atmosphere of a certain uncertainty and danger floating in the air. Thus I decided to rest in a hotel room that day upon my arrival as the following day was supposed to consist of an overall commotion filled with the public appearances. Indran had called and he suggested that we got togerther for breakfast in the hotel's lobby the following day. However, once I put my suitcase down in my hotel room, I started feeling quite restless—in fact, I was eager to get out of the hotel in order to reach the archeological museum which was located in the side of the city oppposite to the hotel's. The receptionist had organised this short trip for me. The ride to the Larco museum took more than an hour as the cab was struggling to get through the oddest suburbs I have ever seen in my life.

True, I was not visiting many of these so called third-world countries recently, but the dissolution of the urban system here followed by the visible confusion of the population have reminded me of my last trip to Cairo. The taxi driver who took me to the museum insisted that he remains in front of the building and wait for me to come out of it as he put it "one never knows what would happen in this part of the city". The same type of advice which sounded like a warning to me I had previously heard from the main organiser of the festival, Renato Sandoval, who, though invisible until that present moment, had called the hotel upon my arrival just to tell me that he was *naturalmente too busy* to greet all of the participants in person but that he cared for our safety and well-being. He was a typically relaxed Latino, quite organized but "el tipo suave" who did not fail to mention the fact "We will all see each other tomorrow" in that soft, nasal latin-american accent of his which suddenly evoked those crazy cocaine New York parties which I attended in the late 1980s.

Luckily, I was not eager any longer to explore all those aspects of the original Indian culture. I thought to myself while hanging down the receiver after Renato's call. I did not like cocaine that much as it was making me terribly sweaty and nervous, moons ago, in quite a distant and different country in which I used to be... quite a different person from the one I considered myself to be nowadays.

However, the total triumph of my ugly reason and reasoning over that substance we call "emotions" has reflected itself within my new and totally pre-meditated approach to themes in my own writing. The themes and so called subjects were not coming spontaneously to me as I would now rather elaborately impose them over spontaneous "accidents" and incidental ideas which I had cherished before... which also meant I gained a totally new style. I was studying certain areas of human knowledge, deeply, in order to write about certain phenomena.

The imposition of a certain thematic choice over yet another turned out to be a practice which the reasonable GUA imposed on that intuitive, natural being. By doing so it tortured and suffocated the instinctual development of the natural being with such learned working practice.

However, the sensitive *Gua* in me had suffered enormously this victory of reason over emotions (as exemplified in the sudden rejection on my part of the advances of that virtuoso violin teacher). It was, (simply put) as if the symphonically oriented Wagner had to tear that oversensitive avant-garde soloist-composer apart and more than several times at once...

I do not know if this innermost testimony makes here any sense. I just want to say that I have arrived here, to this crazy Baroque hotel in order to push all these unreasonable but quite reasonable events far away from me and away from my life. Not that I would forget all these events altogether by deleting them from my memory, but I would somewhat tame them by placing them on a paper, like that particular event for instance: Gera and I, lit up by the dying evening sun, we take a walk down New York's Avenue C, winter time and the Alphabet City!

July 4, 2013

Everything becomes much more clear to me now... I had breakfast with Indran whom I haven't seen some good twenty years. In the meantime- he became the ambassador of the United States in Lima, which means that if I accepted his courtship twenty years ago, perhaps I would have been the U.S. ambassador's wife in Peru today.

However, it appears that we are all the participants of this festival, us, faces from the past, creatures from this present moment and figures of the future which is going to be exclusively mine and joyful, I decided for once and all!

Whatever happens next, one thing soon and then I'll go to the "museum of Gold" so that I can learn something from the Incas, and that includes their knowledge about how one exploits the conquered tribes.. They are said to have been ferocious in that respect, they would drink their victims' blood and similar niceties from their court.

The Armenian princess here fell ill and she told me she felt ever grateful that I gave her my box of aspirins. I retorted that I would do even more for her if I could, my heart totally moved from the story about the Turkish genocide committed over the Armenians earlier in the 20th century. See, what could I do for her? Oh yes, I could persuade Chris Aram to publish the anthology of the contemporary Armenian poetry in English. The Ottomans, as the history goes, massacred more Armenians than us Slavs, in recent history.

I would not dream of taking any photographs here or making any films or videos for that matter. Once upon a time, upon my return from the U.S. to Europe in the late 1990s, I proposed to a friend, a cameraman named Artemio, to take a trip to Latin America with me and film all the "moving images" around us. He was not interested to do it, he simply told me: "See, someone has to remain in Europe as the living is the most difficult around here! I don't want to hear the words such as "resist" and "resistence", because on this territory the most of the human blood has been spilt, we have been fed all of that universal bullshit and the people have been acting around here in the most sensitive and reasonable manner."

HE WAS RIGHT IN ALL THAT.

And then we had quickly and suddenly to move all of us, to a different hotel. I will never know if the cause of this quick move had something to do with the climate in Peru or with the organiser Renato and his mafioso organisation but the fact is that we had to pack our suitcases rather quickly and then, under the dramatic circumstances, move to a different hotel. It had to be done really quickly, between two poetry readings, one of them was scheduled in the National Library and the other one...well I cannot remember where it was.

I was scheduled to read last in the crowd of twenty international poets and when my turn arrived, a macho voice of an organiser gave me an order to cut my reading short, make it snappy.

I was so angry that I felt tears overflowing my eyes and nostrils—and then it stopped!

A local poet named Manuel XYZ tried to dry my tears and took me for a walk through a bohemian quarter Barranco, which is some sort of cool downtown space like Skadarlija in my native Belgrade. He was taking me through that lovely quarter back and forth and in a local café cum beer bar he even tried to plant a kiss on my tired lips.

I cheered up a bit!

Some time ago I gave to a young stud who worked at

the reception desk a twenty euro note to buy us a bit of that famous Colombian coke but the youngster had put the money into his pocket and then pretended that he had never seen me before.

It was a pure set up, so easy to be duped around here. However, when I tried to communicate this event in all my confidentiality to a young Myra, an organiser as well and to the Armenian poet who got the aspirins from me—both of them laughed it off; they seemed proud of their own worldliness and both just kept repeating to me "You are not supposed to deal with things that way around here", they were devoid of any sympathy or remorse for me.

However, what both of these ladies didn't know how to do the following day—was to read their own respective poems in front of a large public.

During the grand inaugural evening of the festival the following evening, each poet from every respective country was supposed to read his own work in front of 5000 people..

Now it was my turn to whisper "You are not supposed to deal with things that way around here"...

It was altogether a beautiful evening. I dared mention to the organiser, Renato, that I did not make a good performer when I was left to read in the very end of the reading. He took my complaint into consideration.

I also dared read my poems translated into Spanish, oh yes, that was quite brave, I have always been brave and with my proverbial courage—I visited half of the globe counting just on my courage—I dared buy three Alpaca sweaters for my son, then I visited that famous museum of Gold where all the exhibits, all the objects in there show an incredible trace and exercise in motherly love. Yes, they were made with an excessive care of motherly attention.

Think, I want you to think now: what would a mother give to a son, more precisely a "conquistador" to whom she was saying good-bye for the very last time in her life while at the same time being aware, conscious of the fact that she might never ever see him again? She would give him the nicest, the most ornate cross made of gold, as well as a piece of her bleeding heart (Spanish and Portugese Baroque).

And how did the Indians from the Ketchua tribe bury their dead? They mumified them,and their mothers with their babies, I'd never know if the mothers die first and then the babies or the babies had gone first then the members of the tribe killed their mothers—who would trace their individual stories yet in this museum full of golden statues and mummies?

And then in the same museum rooms we see the tons of arms, tons of arms which belonged to the conquerors.. they stand against the background of the mummiefied mothers with their forlorn babies and executed sons.

I have collected quite a large amount of material for our Latin American issue of (Giancarlo's and my own) magazine “Niemand Rose”.

For the first time here I fell asleep like a newborn, I fell asleep like an angel on Friday and I got up like a real human being on Saturday.

It already reads JULY 6, and it is the end of my trip

What I am going to say is not probably anything new for neuroscience but it’s a mindblowing thing to my simple mini-me. I have observed my brain (I took a good distance), and it seemed to me that switching from one language to another, or from one culture, or civilization to another—is exactly like changing different computer programs. As if I entirely have transferred here to the “Spanish civilization” program—all of a sudden I was plugged onto that program, I chatted with my collegues in Spanish, collecting their books, even interviewing some of them—all in Spanish, the language which I believed I had forgotten, some twenty years ago.

I interviewed a Chilean poet, Sergio B., whose life resembled a bit my own, strange and fragmented, meandering in all parts of Europe, and then after some good thirty years of living abroad—he returned to his homecountry which is Chile!

He tried to explain to me the intricate history of the Peruvuan and Chilean relationship, as we were walking through the center of Lima with Henrietta, yet another poet from Sweden who happens to live in Finland! We ran into some kids in the street while these were playing football and Sergio was adamant to ask them some questions, only to illustrate his testimony about the Peruvian-Chilean relations which he earlier made to us.

"Kids," he asked them, "where do you think I come from?"

The kids had replied in one voice "From Spain, sir, you surely come from Spain".

"Oh, no, you're wrong," he exclaimed."I come from the worst country in the world! What is it?"

"Chile, Chile!" all these kids started screaming.

These countries were the old enemies. Sergio says that he is obliged to speak the Argentinian accent in the streets of Peru so that the passers by would not throw rotten vegetables at him.. terrible but a likely story, as I had a somewhat similar experience in the streets of Dubrovnik, after the Serbian and Croatian civil wars, during the last decade of the twentieth century...

So we continued walking along these *conquistador* rococo streets among the buildings where one could find the most grinding poverty of all shantytowns and underprivilegded suburbs. No, nothing bad will happen to me here, but on the other hand—nothing good was meant to happen either. Here, everyone is well-trained to take advantage of blue-eyed gringas.

I was more than aware there of that latin american seduction, of that particular charm of the patriarchal seducer—well, this very evening at that very square Barranca—where my Latino collegue Miguel tried to jump at me—at that very place we read poetry in the open, it was only thirteen Celsius degrees, lots of fresh air and no fresh water to drink after the reading.

The organiser has invited 114 poets but the entire organisational efforts went beyond his original planning and expectations. We went back to the hotel to warm up a little bit and in there they served that special agawa drink, the so called local *pisco.* Sweet and made of extraordinary strong alcohol brew, pisco goes right into one's head and usually people faint and fall down after consuming one or two shots of it. So I sort of fainted and fell down.

However, before I finally fell down and fainted, I recall taking the Chilean Sergio into my room where I intended to give him copies of my books, and that was it, indeed. He misunderstood my invitation and collegial gesture and as soon as he stepped into my hotel room, he started taking his clothes off and then lied down in my bed without any further explanation or intention to tell me why he'd behave that way. Like in some soft Almodovar's movie I ran out of that suite, and started knocking at the door number 313, which hid behind an incredibly civilized and cultured Madrilleno, a Spanish poet Raul Campo.

Hola, Raul, please help me, come to my rescue. There is a certain poet who came to my room and lied down in my bed and in fact, I did not even invite him to join me, and now, he has no intention to leave my room...

Elegant creature Raul invited the unbearable poet

Sergio to come out and go down with him to the bar where they were supposed to have yet another pisco, but the story gets a bit rough and raggedy at this point as I fell down the stairs and now regained my bed..Renato the organiser and his drinking pals from the bar have took me to the second floor, I was completely unconscious, "that happens often to poets here", someone was mumbling in the background.

July 7, Lima

At any rate, one could never say for this city that it was boring. The following day, I woke up rather early despite that bad hangover from the previous night, only to hear my own voice clear and loud in Spanish. These sounds were coming from the local loudspeaker but were recorded the previous evening—these were my poems which my friend Sacha had translated beautifully—I could tell the translations were good by the overwhelming laughter coming from the international poets and the rest of the crowd. One long hurray for Sacha who translated them and even louder hurray for me who wrote them.

"Where have you learnt to speak such good Spanish?" the oldest poet from Argentina, Guillermo Ariel, had asked me, and was totally surprised to hear my response. Juan Octavio Prens, his old collegue and one of his best childhood friends was teaching classes in Spanish civilization at the University of Belgrade. "Ha, the world is small but not always predictable," Guillermo said and then added "thank you, poet, for letting me know where my best friend exiled himself, I was looking for him for the last 30 years!"

July 8

The world is rather small and it contracts even further as we go around it—on Saturday—and that was the day of the closing of the festival, I met at the entrance the local poet Manuel Leido and his wife. He was in the midst of the dispute with her as he was desperately trying to explain to her where he spent the last two days in Lima, he said he was a part of the festival but she did not quite believe him. Now, I came as a remedy, so to speak.

He obviously cheered up when he spotted me and said: "Nina, Sylvia is my old friend and she had ordered me over the phone to take care of you! In fact, we Skyped one another two days ago and I told her that the festival hosted a fabulous Serbian poet, Nina, who also had lived in New York!" Sylvia and Frank were my old friends from New York, she was from Lima, he was from the Lower East Side in New York City—Frank was a great painter for whom I organised several shows in Paris, among other things—I miss them dearly.

I reassured the Peruvian poet and his wife that they

were not in charge of my life—in fact, no one had to take care of me, but it was very sweet and friendly that Sylvia worried about me. That evening, a Ketchua poet named Luis took me to the port ending with a long beach, as I had previously told him that my only desire was to see the ocean, that is the Pacific, as I had a strange premonition that I was not going to see it again. As we were walking down the beach, all of a sudden, I saw Chris's face in the fog rising above us.

Strange creature, my British editor—once he discovered the key which opened my mind's door, he would predict every action of mine, he was reading my mind, like you read a novel. And that novel of my mind he published himself, in one of his collections.

For who else, but my British editor would make a joke like this one "The Farcs were quite fortunate this time as they failed to kidnap you—you are such a troublemaker, Nina!" And I was, indeed. I'm just hoping that the consumption of that wicked drink, pisco, did not chase my persona out of his heart. Last night I used the hotel phone and called him—in England, it must had been quite a late hour but he himself said it once, "You can call me any time, really any hour you want."

The next morning, I totally sobered when I had to pay the bills at the reception desk—my debt to the country of the poor had to be reimbursed—the small bar in the hotel cost a lot of money, but perhaps, that WAS the last time I used it there....

Nina Živančević published her first book in 1982 for which she won the National Award for poetry in Yugoslavia. From 1980 to 1981 she worked as a teaching assistant and secretary to Allen Ginsberg. She worked as a literary editor for *East Village Eye* and *Theater X*, a freelance journalist for *Politika*, *El Pais*, *L'Unita*, *Woman* (Spain), and *Nexus*, and as a contributor to *The New Yorker* and *New York Arts Magazine*. Besides having performed with The Living Theater (1988-1992) and La Mama Experimental Theatre Club, she co-founded in 1988 the Odiyana Theatre. She is author of more than twenty books and has translated notable works of poetry into Serbian. In 2001 she completed her PhD in Comparative Literature and Slavic Studies at Université Nancy 2 with a thesis on the modernist literature of Serbian writer Miloš Crnjanski. That same year she contributed the text "Pandora's Box" to the Semiotext(e) reader *Hatred of Capitalism*, in which she addresses the war in Yugoslavia, and in relation to which she worked in 1996 as an official Serbian, Croatian and Bosnian translator for the International Tribunal for War Crimes at the Hague. In 2002 she received a Special Grant from the American PEN association of writers presided by Robert Creeley. She presently serves on the editorial committee of the journal *Au Sud de l'Est*. She lives in Paris and teaches languages and the theatre of the avant-gardes at Paris University.

www.ingramcontent.com/pod-product-compliance
Lightning Source LLC
Chambersburg PA
CBHW061619190726
48288CB00007B/2391

* 9 7 8 1 9 5 9 5 5 6 2 9 9 *